Many people become debilitated through stress. Overtime, unmanaged stress may create problems in relationships, and in work environments, it can manifest itself and create headaches, illness, heart problems and death.

Hypothesis for Writing This Book:

By identifying the stressor relating to a person experiencing stress, the stress can be managed. Manging stress allows the student to successfully sit the examination, the doctor to perform surgery, the farmer to successfully run his farm or the business owner to successfully run their business.

We support Diabetes Type One, Cancer Research and Motor Neuron Disease. 10% of the net sales will be divided equally between our charities.

You cannot reduce stress if you don't know how to Work with Your Mind.

Regardless of the hurdles you are facing, you have the ability to learn how to Work Your Mind, aim for your targets, reach your goals, live the life you want to live, make the choices you want to make, create your own wellbeing and to become fully self-sustainable!

The main objective of your human mind and spirit is to learn, grow and survive.

Unmanaged stress is a time bomb waiting to explode!

LEARNING TO WORK WITH YOUR MIND…

Reduce Stress

Learn To Work With Your Mind and

Discover:
Your Aliveness

Your Emotional Intelligence

Your Three Ego Personality States And
The Role They Play In Your Life

Discover The Four Orders Within *Self,* Family And Work

Your Mind, Body and Spirit And

The Working Components Of Your Mind &
Your Centre Of Intelligence

Is it possible, the Human Mind has so much power it can
create a new and better place for humans to live, thrive and
develop? Can we make a sustainable future for our future
generations?

Disclaimer

This is not a medical book and should not be used as such. The contents have been developed through observational theory and research (observational psychology). Information is also drawn from scientific literature, web search and personal enquiry. While all care is taken, the information is not warranted as accurate. Additive numbers, E Numbers and ISN numbers are continually changing and being updated. At the time of writing this book, the Additive Numbers were current.

The diagrams are for information and to enhance the meaning of the written text.

Statements, information, and ideas within this book are for education purposes only. The text presented allows the reader to draw their own conclusions on the content offered.

Always consult with your doctor for possible illness or underlying illness.

Before dietary investigation, consult a dietician with an interest in food intolerance or food related diseases and disorders.

Christine Thompson-Wells (MSI) Australia and Books For Reading On Line.Com, cannot be held liable for any errors or omissions.

ISBN: 978-0-6481884-7-6

Published by Books For Reading On Line.Com.,
under license from MSI Ltd, Australia
Company Registration No: 64293859
New South Wales, Australia

See our website: *www.booksforreadingonline.com*

Or contact by email: sales@booksforreadingonline.com
Front & Back Covers and Copyright owned by MSI, Australia

Christine Thompson-Wells, Lifestyle Psychologist and Book Author of many books which include:

39 Days & 39 Days To Debt Recovery

Making Cash Flow

How To Reduce Stress

How To Reduce Anxiety

Discover Your Selling Power

Beat Stress – Find Your Positive Headspace

Make Your Money Work

A Series Of Whispering Books For Relaxation And Reduce Stress

Devils In Our Food – Devils In Our Food Handbook, Recipes Without Devils, Devils In Our Food Audio Book

The Golden Book of Poetry and many other titles.

And many featured articles in the national print media of the United Kingdom. She has been a regular guest speaker for BBC national radio and guest appearance for the Politics Show, BBC Television.

How to *Reduce Stress* takes evidence-based psychology to the maximum. The research for the books: *How To Reduce Stress* and *How To Reduce Anxiety* (soon to be released) spans over forty years of dedication to the topics covered. Christine Thompson-Wells has been an active writer for many years and went to the University of Canberra, Australia while her children were small.

Over an eleven to twelve-year span and while at university, Christine studied Adult Education majoring in Psychology; and is in further advanced studies.

Christine is the author of many published books, national magazine and newspaper articles incorporating money psychology and has said: *'money psychology is the study of people's behaviour when working with and managing money...'*

Having moved on from money psychology but still incorporating the subject, Christine now writes about the total human being using a diverse range of studies which cover the experiences of many people. She has now developed the area of Lifestyle Psychology.

The eleven case studies held within *How To Reduce Stress* show a sample of how human thinking and action, influence human activity worldwide; the book also identifies how *stress* can be managed once the right mental tools are in place.

While collecting the information, Christine has owned and run businesses, taught, and lectured in schools, colleges, and university; counselled young offenders in the prison system, and had short-term contracts in the public sector as a researcher.

She has researched her work from education to publishing and other industries. The studies include retail and the fitness industries and other areas of human interaction. She has briefly known some of the people in the studies while in other areas, a deep analysis and long-term investigation has taken place.

Because there is always a call from her mind to write; she gathers new research from new environments of education, industry, corporate, commerce and life, then writes up the information she has learnt and moves on to the next calling.

Christine is a qualified educator and teacher; she specialises as a Lifestyle psychologist and, as a writer, she writes from many Psychological approaches and disciplines. She has been a constant source of information and speaks live on BBC radio, television and writes in the print media of the United Kingdom.

She is a mother, wife, and businesswoman and above all, a human being.

Your Mind Gearbox – you can change gears at any time!

This book incorporates the respected work of Eric Berne[1] and his identification of the human Ego Personality States. I also include Emotional Intelligence, love, hate and revenge; the interpretations, individual differences, social behaviours, and educational psychology; different ideas combining human attitudes and behaviours, *stress* inoculation and the *Stress Monitor*.

For the first time, I have identified, your valuable *Centre of Intelligence*.

Your mind is your Mental Gearbox; for a successful life, you need to know how to drive your mind and what gear you are driving in! I introduce you to this fascinating concept and expand on it in my next book, *How To Reduce Anxiety.*

Christine Thompson-Wells

Lecturer & teacher in Lifestyle Psychology, specialising in Human Relations, Communications and Money Psychology, Internationally Accredited Educator, CPD Trainer & Facilitator

---

[1] Berne, Eric (1964) The Games People Play

The interpretations of the case studies held within this book are interpretations and points of view. There are many factors, as you will discover, that contribute to different people, their thinking, behaviour, and the stress they experience.

The writings which follow are meant to be taken as self-help, human development tools. Each reader will take from the text their own interpretation and use the mental tools they develop accordingly.

In How To Reduce Stress – I have used the biblical character names of Adam and Eve to allow for easy identification within the studies.

Christine

Dedicated to my family

And the readers of this book.

Introduction

Stress is underlying and intrinsic within the human system and psychology – psychology is the study of human behaviour. We, as individuals, need moderate amounts of good stress to do our daily chores and to survive. In the fast-moving twenty-first century, more people are experiencing negative or bad stress. I have written this book to allow you to develop the mental tools which will let you work with and manage many areas of stress in your life.

Whether by accident or trial and error, the human species found that cooked food was better for them than roar – this time in our evolution seems to point to a leap forward in thinking, action and development of the human being. To be able to think, take action, and have outcomes from the efforts put into place was indeed the birth of psychology. By thinking things through it allowed human beings to survive and become the people we are today.

This book incorporates the impact of stress and the effects it has on you, the actions you take and the outcomes you work with – this is after all, human behaviour – possibly, your behaviour which may incorporate the stress you experience!

Psychology is a fascinating subject, that is with us from being a newly born infant, to the time we lie on our deathbed, we use psychology everyday of our lives.

From living in an isolated community in remote parts of the world to living and existing in large cities – we all use psychology and experience some form of stress every waking minute of our lives.

Some people use psychology and negative stress to detrimental results as in terrorism, and some use psychology and positive stress for only good outcomes; these people include doctors, care workers and those people helping the victims who suffer from injuries in war-torn countries and those people who work with people suffering from deadly diseases such as the Ebola virus and in the Covid pandemic.

Psychology is used, without exception, by everybody in every action they do and every word they speak. Psychology is used by hairdressers, dentists, council employees and the people who have dedicated their lives searching for cures to human, flora and animal diseases. Psychology is used in the classroom, the lecture theatre, schooling, and education, in the factory and in the fields while the farmer is gathering in his crops!

Psychology is used in manufacturing, heavy industry, shipping, travel, marketing, mining, crime, crime prevention, entertainment, in film and television production, banking, finance, the prison system, to the baker baking bread and the gaming industry – every facet of human behaviour incorporates the use of psychology and a form of stress being either negative or positive.

The title of *Adam's Mind – Eve's Psyche* was the original book title for this book, however, through the evolution of the writing,

I have divided this first book into two parts and these parts have become the books: *How To Reduce Stress* and *How To Reduce Anxiety (still to be printed)*. Thus, this division has allowed me to focus more on two separate areas of human behaviour, these being *Stress* and *Anxiety*. Taking each area separately will help you to understand your emotional intelligence and the mental drivers that we all use while we are living our everyday lives.

This first book *How To Reduce Stress,* shows you how to apply your mind and the ability you have to bring about a win-win outcome with life situations. The book allows you to develop new, recognisable mind-tools that lead to workable mind-skills that in turn will increase your quality of life and reduce your stress. It allows the young mum to see the difference when working with and nursing her new-born baby; it asks the executive of a major corporation to look a little deeper when faced with making major decisions; to the politician working on policy changes in the government, to the woman who has a dream of education for her children and for the pensioner who knows that life has more to offer!

Preface

Psychology is taking on a mainstream application as schools, colleges, universities, government, the military and employers see the benefits to their organisation once there is an understanding of how the human mind operates within different environments and with changing life conditions.

We live in a rapidly moving and changing society that affects us all. At different times, we find, we have, to manage situations and conditions that change our lives forever; these changes all incorporate psychology and different levels of stress.

We all need to develop mind-tools, mind-skills, and stress management strategies to be able to adapt quickly which will allow us to have the ability to make changes when we need to.

Most human beings want a fairer and equitable society to live within; they want to know that people have equal opportunities for education, health, and life prospects. Positive changes will be made through education and the understanding that all people have good minds; it is in how they use and manage the mind that makes the difference!

When you add to the mix – each person uses their mind differently, then, mix in emotional intelligence, the three ego states of Parent, Adult, Child and some stress, the journey becomes an exciting adventure, and at times, a little *hell raising!*

The objective of this book is to allow you the thinking time to develop your mind-tools, mind-skills and physical abilities, which in turn will allow you to make the changes you want to make. This will add quality to your life and give you the inspiration to reach your full potential.

Within the book, I have used a story approach to the studies to keep the action and dynamics of the words moving, thus invigorating you to read the valuable information that is held on every page.

I have mentioned in previous books, The journey has been long and for over the forty years I have been building the manuscripts, (some of the case studies are contained within this book and other books I have written), many people have contributed. Sadly, some are now deceased but it is with their legacy that I have been able to draw on the experience of talking with them and experiencing their story that has allowed me to bring these books together.

I thank all the people who have supported me with their input of information. I also want to thank those people who thought and said: *'it would not happen!'*

There are many people who do not understand how the human mind works and how human determination can conquer great feats. Thank you to those people also. If I had only received praise during the working process of my writings, my determination would have diminished years ago!

Unmanaged
stress is a
time bomb
waiting to
explode!

What Is Stress?

Meichenbaum[2] – his assumption being: '... *stress is caused by faulty processing of information ...*'

Thompson-Wells *'Destructive stress in your mind and body is the negative reaction to the situation you are experiencing.'*

[2] Meichenbaum, Coping With Stress (1972). Thompson-Wells, Adam's Mind – Eve's Psyche (2014)

Content   **Page**

- The power of the human mind should not be underestimated
- Personal contracts – human contracts
- If you do not intend to keep the contract on the following page, please do not sign it
- The Contract
- Your notes

Chapter Seven 136
Emotional Intelligence, Personal Contracts, Self, Family and Work

- The Beginning of understanding emotional intelligence and the Orders within Self, Family and Work
- There is always a lot going on inside your head!
- A progression of thinking
- Taking the initiative
- Eve
- Eve continually works with her Adult ego personality state and her positive emotional intelligence
- Eve's best friend
- It is the start of understanding – Eve and her friend
- Emotional intelligence
- Self, Family and Work
- Emotional intelligence and their three symbolic, figurative shapes
- Emotional intelligence within Self, Family and Work
- Starting with Self
- Self
- Family
- Work
- Introducing your emotional intelligence, Self, Family, Work and their Four Orders – First Order
- Self – First Order
- Self – First Order – Family
- Natural Law
- Self – First Order – Work
- Using change in your life – you may wish to come back to this later in the book
- Your notes

- Working in the Fourth Order
- The obedient servant – the human brain and mind
- Under the most severe of circumstances, we can each work in a positive and constructive direction – working with the Fourth Order
- Living in the Fourth Order
- Self and Family
- Your notes

- Getting inside your head
- Reactivity vs proactivity
- Proactivity – driving your mind
- First gear
- Second gear
- Third gear
- Fourth gear
- Reverse
- The goldmine inside your head
- Your mind of gold and your Centre of Intelligence
- They are there and ready to use
- Learning how to breathe
- Extracted from my book 'Go' Success is Yours
- Managing stress – Work
- The stress guide and monitor – in Work
- The stress guide
- First stage – cognitive preparation
- Second stage – skill acquisition and coping strategies including thought restructuring
- Third stage – application and following through
- Stress inoculation
- Thought restructuring
- Breathing properly and thought restructuring
- Now, your upper body to your lower body
- Identify your work performance and stress levels

- Other options
- A technique in quickly managing stress
- Your gearbox inside your head – now you know you have it, there is no excuse not to use it!
- Your notes

Managing your stress

Unmanaged stress is a time bomb waiting to explode!

Chapter One

Mind Altering Substances, Co-dependency, and Learned Helplessness

Many people camouflage their stress through smoking cigarettes, drinking alcohol, and taking drugs. Because many people start using substances, which help to develop bad habits when they are young, they are not fine-tuned to what their body is telling them. They may not realise they are in stress and may have been living with severe stress for most of their adult life. When habit forming substances are combined with anger and frustration, it can become a toxic, and evil combination within any human system.

It is not always easy to stop or slow down once a body's system has become anesthetized to ingested or used chemicals. Your body has not got used to it, your brain has accepted it because the chemical or substance is constantly in your system. Your body simply learns to work with the condition it is forced to work with until one day, the substance or chemical has done so much damage, the body gives up under the strain and this is shown through the behaviour a person exhibits when they become unwell. While taking different chemical substances, a person may feel relieved at the intake of the substance but once the substance or chemical is in the body, the person will develop a form of stress to manage the ingredients.[3]

---

[3] Many substances are administered to the human system when a condition or illness needs to be managed. Taking drugs for the kick of taking the drug, smoking cigarettes or the overuse of alcohol not only damages the liver, kidneys, and other areas of the human body, but also the human brain.

The aim of the words written in this book are to alert, and to give you the mental tools that will provide a deeper, more meaningful, quality-filled, and prosperous life.

Prosperity is not always measured in the form of money or wealth but life prosperity may come in the quality and richness of the life which you live; on the other hand, it's nice to know that the power of your mind can help you to create your wealth. Creating what you want or want to achieve is part of your distinctiveness. It is the distinctiveness and originality of each, and every person's mind that this book is about.

As I have often said, 'each, and every one of us is unique; some of us are born, similar, but no one is identical!' At the time of your birth, you brought with you something that had not existed before nor shall exist again; you brought your distinctiveness, your uniqueness and originality. These differences are what makes you, you. Sadly, many people suffer through uncontrolled *stress* which interferes with their distinctiveness.

Throughout life, you may have many opportunities to work with your distinctiveness, to make an impression, to leave your footprint of accumulated knowledge, or you have the choice to do nothing. Stress may lead you on to do nothing when an opportunity presents itself. Doing nothing is not an option, the only option is to become a winner and to go for the opportunity if it feels right for you.

Sadly, many people die without taking up opportunities. Stress can be a killer of challenge. Challenge is part of the great human potential that we all possess Many people die not having fulfilled their greatest human potential. They have not developed or made

2

the most of their marvellous mind, the availability of their talents or developed their skills, or used their distinctiveness to its maximum advantage – they may have indeed, wasted their life!

To avoid this dilemma, when understanding how stress plays a strategic role in your life, you, are able, to manage many of the challenges you will face as you make your life journey.

By understanding this concept, the child born today, and given this knowledge, is a winner in the future.

We are all born with a clean slate; we do not have troublesome thoughts or baggage from a past; we are indeed whole and a mentally clean tiny human being.

Not all children, come into loving families, or families that are free from worry. Many parents are facing troublesome times without homes or countries to call their own. Some children are orphaned from an early age, but some are more fortunate and come into safety and security.

From your inception and while awaiting your birth, you started to accumulate information; this incoming information is stored in your memory and is used as base data throughout your life span. You soon learnt, while in the womb, that it is comforting to suck your thumb, grab your toes and explore your body, and possibly seeing, the faint light of daylight shining through your mother's skin.

During this time, you learnt to listen to the sounds from outside the womb and around you and, to your mother's voice, her heartbeat, even the music she may have danced to! This was the beginning of your exploration and the adaption of your developing senses and was part of getting to know what was going on in your world.

For us all, at birth, we are all born equal, some only equal for a few seconds but we are all born as an innocent baby. Research is showing that children born into stressful environments, do develop many different forms of trauma and stress. And, indeed, many adults experiencing stress, may be sick from stress but do not realise they are sick.

It is painful to think that some people, through culture, customs, ignorance, lack of education or a belief system they are initiated into, or without human rights, do indeed miss out in their potential life opportunities. Each, and every situation we experience all relate to our body and mind going through different forms of stress. I will explain the different forms of stress as you go through the book.

It's the adults of today that have the power and influence to change not only their own life for the better but the lives of their children, grandchildren, nieces, nephews, cousins, neighbours and other people they are connected to or communicate with, within their community.

As adults, we, can learn to work with stressful situations. We can also teach our children how to manage different stressful times and this education will support your child as they journey through their life.

Changing lives for the better is not done through drumming information into someone's head – this is manipulation and is not what this book is about.

By understanding how stress works and gaining positive information, knowledge, and the acknowledgement of your own mental capacity and capability, you can change your life for the better.

The human brain is a magnificent piece of human technology that has great strength and capacity. Many of life's experiences are challenging and are stressful times. It is, however, the way we manage those times that make the difference. The brain is a large grey and white organ that sits within your skull. This brain, when treated with respect, can be used to great advantage, and if used wisely, it can add benefits to your life and to the wellbeing of all people throughout the world.

This book is a journey of discovery, it is the facilitator of the voyage and the vehicle to work with you that you use daily that takes you into your future.

If you are into discovery, then please keep reading. The reading will lead you into positive changes, better health, less *negative stress,* and personal growth.

Changing how you think

Many people who want change, who want to make change do not necessarily look for the fastest route but for the most genuine route for their journey. Managing stress is about knowing the journey you are on and if the journey does not take you to where you want to go you, can change direction!

In life, the journey needs to be worthwhile and have purpose. Purpose is what the words on these pages are about. When you are on a genuine journey, you feel the reliability that is within your inner-self; you feel the energy within and you know you have the confidence to see your journey through – you are working with a surge of *positive stress*. Positive stress allows you to see the pathway and journey ahead.

Working with positive stress allows you take the opportunity and allows you to see if you are travelling in the right direction to reach your goal or goals.

A traumatic journey

New Zealand Massacre

With two consecutive shootings in New Zealand, a sole Australian gunman killed 51 people, including one child, at an attack on two different mosques. Janna Ezat, mother of Hussein Al-Umari while he knelt in prayer at 12.01 on 15th March 2019, was shot and killed. At his trial, Ms. Ezat, publicly forgave 29-year-old Brenton Tarrant.[4]

Ms. Ezat, knew to carry the grief she was experiencing would not bring her beautiful boy home or back to her. The time of grief for a child is a time no parent ever wants to go through. By publicly showing her forgiveness, she was releasing some of her possible

---

[4] https://www.thetimes.co.uk

anger and pain, therefore, she is releasing some of the stress that is attached to both.

Ms. Ezat, was and is possibly still coming from the genuine inner self of her personality.

To have such courage shows she will not let herself down. Ms. Ezat, is self-actualizing that is reliable and dependable.

Though she may not realise, Ms. Ezat, shows she is connected to her family, neighbourhood, and the community in which she lives. This lady is unique and dedicated, though she still feels the pain, and has the pain and memories of her child as a little boy and the loss of her child she works with the pain during the time of forgiveness. Such human strength takes fortitude to show, and the use of *positive stress* to manage her feelings, emotions, and her life as it is now.

The gears of your mind

As you read through the book, I talk about your mind and the gears of your mind that you can work with. The mind gearbox, and mind gears, are similar, to the gears we use when we decide to drive our cars. The only difference with mind gears, we cannot see them because they are there inside our heads. When driving our vehicles, we can see what gear we are using. If the gear is in neutral, we are stationary, we are not about to go anywhere, but when the car gear is put into action, we reach our destination.

Going nowhere, is not the purpose you were born. You have a purpose, and it is your responsibility to find your purpose!

Being in positive mental gear is the only gear to work in. When you are in your genuine *mental gear* you are working with the world as it is. You do not think of going into any fantasy world of:

- *maybe!*
- *what if?* or
- *should be!*

Sometimes we need to take our time before making big commitments to a life challenge. We need to wait-and-see. During these times, we may need to consolidate our ideas and experiences before making the decision. While enduring these experiences, our body and mind can experience a lot of stress.

Having said this, when we are in the 'real world' we remain objective and focused on the journey undertaken – this, Dr Eric Berne described as the '*Adult Ego Personality State.*'

A person who is genuine to themselves will be learning from the pain or journey they are experiencing. They are not frivolous with their time or waste valuable energy and time to want to punish or to manipulate others. These people want real outcomes to a real purpose.

With all of the above said, people who experience such awful pain as a mother, regardless of the age of the child, will have their time of great sorrow and pain but they will eventually come through this experience and eventually find the light.

When our ten-year-old son was diagnosed with Diabetes Type One or Juvenile Onset Diabetes, all colour went from the world around me and went from my vision. I now realise, this was due to the stress I was experiencing.

When working positively with stress, and with the mental tools of managing stress, the time it takes to heal will be understood and the journey will be a time of great growth and personal repair. We each learn in our own way and on our own journey.

Having said this, as you will find out, that repairing takes time, but you will eventually learn to play, have fun, and thoroughly enjoy your life and the journey you are travelling. You will identify your own weakness and strengths but more than that, you will live in the real world. When you live in the real world you are not living in the artificial world of make believe and the celebrity image.

You take responsibility for the words you say and the actions you take. By understanding, not only your stress levels but also how your physiology[5] and mind work together.

When you are working positively with your brain, mind and your body's physiology, you listen to others – you collect the required information or data, you also want to know other ways; you only want to collect the incoming information that is relevant and makes good sense. You want the information that you can channel to your mind, process it, wait, take time to digest the information or data, use your past experiences, some from early childhood, to make up your mind.

---

[5] Human physiology is the study of human organs, and of the cells that make them up. An understanding of human physiology is helpful in a variety of fields, such as medicine, fitness, and biology.

You use timing and will only respond when the time is right and fits the appropriate situation – only then, will you take-action.

Because of the respect you have for you as a person, you do not waste time; you use time to its maximum advantage. You also understand that each moment contributes to the time you spend constructively each-and-every day.

Wrong turns

Even the most level-headed of people do make wrong turns in life. Sometimes, we are faced with a situation we were not prepared for. These wrong turns are not times for lamentations or blame of yourself. These times are for your learning and for toughening up. These times are getting you ready for the next journey in your life.

Though you may have learned a lot in your life, you feel, while living, the learning continues. People who have had great hardship at a young age, continue, to grow, and learn. Learning is life-long.

The learning we do today, though it might be stressful, creates the survival mechanisms we will need for the future.

The importance of the message here is: though you maybe, experiencing stress today, learn from the experience but on the journey do not forget to work, rest, when to take-action, and play. Life does and will always have its challenges and with each challenge there will be a degree of stress attached. It is knowing how to manage the attached stress accordingly to each situation that counts.

Each new day presents its own unique situation. Each new day is a discovery, and you are on your journey, life is continually challenging you to manage and work your life's pathway which may include:

- To love and care for an elderly parent
- To nurse a sick child
- To pay the household bills while trying to manage debt
- A sickness to work with
- A death or divorce to get through
- A life to rebuild
- A life changing injury to adjust to, and in
- 2020, to manage the Covid pandemic.

All, of the above and more situations require different stress levels and different thoughts and different actions to take. taken.

Thought for the day:

Janna Ezat, mother of Hessein Al-Umari has shown great strength in the loss of her son which is possibly too difficult for the most of us to comprehend.

Can you give one thought that would allow you to grow and forgive a person or situation?

....

....

....

Daily papers, television, newspaper reports and other media often mention the pain people suffer

Sometimes pain is self-inflicted. Many people create a mess in their life and expect others to help them out or come to the rescue. Many people also create their own co-dependency[6] environment. All such created living environments can create many forms of negative stress.

As I have said, *'when you were born, you were born with a clean slate ...'* and new beginning. Many people are born into a negative environment and grow and learn from that environment. It is not until a person takes on the responsibility to make changes from a negative to a positive mental state will their life change.

In past years, psychology focused on emotions that were negative. Now, there is more emphasis on positive emotion which can strongly influence our levels of happiness which allows other areas of our lives to grow and flourish.

Losing material goods can give you strength to grow

Throughout the world, many people are losing their life's work because of the Covid pandemic.

There are about 7.5 million businesses or more that will close worldwide if the Covid pandemic continues.

---

[6] Is the excessive psychological or emotional reliance on another person through addiction or through excessive emotional or psychological reliance on a partner, or typically one who requires support on account of an illness.

Many people will experience dire financial situations if a vaccine is not found in the foreseeable future. This is a familiar story. Living under such conditions creates stress in the human body.

How to handle or manage these situations is going to lead to learning that people will be forced to do. When a human being is forced to change, not only the way they think and behave but they are forced into looking for different work. Some people may leave their country of their birth, some may take an opportunity that presents itself and some may get into crime. Getting into crime is not a good or positive option. Many people, because of their life situation, (having to provide food, education or rent for the family may push a person into this type of activity). Many may end up in jail. Each of these situations creates many stressors in a person.

If one is persistent, they may find a job that fits with their personality or they may find a job that 'fills the gap' while the world waits for a cure to be found.

Some people will make positive changes in their lives and possibly start working in their own small business and become successful. Each is a time of transition and each transition takes its toll on the individual. Each transition has stress and stressor[7] attached to the situation

---

[7] A stressor is the stimulus (or threat) that causes stress, e.g. the threat of being ill as in the Covid pandemic, exam, divorce, family arguments, death of loved one, moving-house, loss of job and other uncontrollable situations that threaten the human being.

Mike is determined

Including his local and tourist trade and over five years, Mike had worked hard in his gelato shop.

First there were the bush fires, and now the Covid pandemic had hit the world. With many areas off limits for travel, the coastal towns on the Eastern coast of Australia now had restrictions on visitors, in fact, people were told to stay away.

Mike knew that an ice cream and gelato shop were not high on people's list to visit. He was determined he was not going to go out of business so he thought about how could he diversify?

He had decided to create a café with many different foods including take-away lunches and coffee for sale. He also kept his ice creamery going and added different ranges of jams and conserves for people to buy.

Many situations can make us add to our income stream. By making changes, Mike may have reduced his stress load and increased his financial survival.

The Feel Better Box

An enterprising young woman called Sarah found herself out of work. She was also suffering with a heavy cold (not Covid), and felt she needed to cheer herself up. She arranged and bought herself some items to make herself feel better.

By buying some 'feel good' items, it cheered her up and she felt better. This was the start of her enterprising venture. She now has an online business called The Feel Better Box[8] and supplies to people, via online, a range of beautiful gifts, her business is booming.

Losing her job and suffering with a severe head cold allowed Sarah to turn a negative situation into a positive outcome. Through working with positive stress, it allowed Sarah to release the negative stress her body was accumulating. She, now, also employs members of her family to help her out over busy times.

Most, of us, once we realise the good brain inside our heads is there to help us and not hinder us on our life journey, the brain we carry becomes a friend to work with.

Polish slaves - Slave gang trafficked people from Poland to exploit in the UK[9]

Recently seen on television was the documentary about the slave trade uncovered in the United Kingdom. The bosses of the crime-ring were arrested and are now in jail. However, the people, which were at least 400 of them, led a life of misery and squalor. These people lived in abject poverty while their captors lived in luxury and this is all happening in the 21st Century!

Because of threats being made to loved ones or family members, people can learn to live with dire situations – they literally just survive. When a person is subject to extreme mental of physical cruelty, they find a survival mode that fits their situation. Because of fear, people, such as the recently discovered slaves in the

---

[8] https://www.feelbetterbox.com.au
[9] https://www.dailymail.co.uk

United Kingdom learnt to live with threats of being bashed or their families being hurt.

These people did not speak English and knew nothing of their human rights while living in the United Kingdom. Eventually, regardless of the threats made on them, some slaves escaped.

The slave racket was under investigation from the Polish Police and the British Police were part of the surveillance team working on the case.

The stress was seen, though the criminals were now in jail, on the faces of the people as they spoke, through interpreters, about their ideal. Because of the fear factor instilled in the victims, the criminals had absolute power over their slaves.

Recently in this chapter, I have spoken about co-dependency. Co-dependency allowed the criminals to control the people in the above case study. Many people, the world over live in a state of co-dependency. By people being forced to live under such conditions, their stress levels are elevated, they live in fear and live out of personal control.

We know that some people want to have the good things in life handed to them on a plate without the effort it takes to become self-actualised.[10]

---

[10] Self-actualised is the awareness and recognising of personal limits, in addition to focusing on unique strengths, these may include practical skills, artistic capacity, emotional insights and working with inherited talents.

Co-dependency

Co-dependent individual, (in some instances) such as the criminals in the last case study, are those people who live only through the help or support of other people. Most of these people have all that is needed mentally and physically to lead a full and satisfying life.

A co-dependent individual can be a parasite and is always waiting for the silver lining, the winning lottery ticket, the next scam, or criminal act they can commit at the expense of others.

Learned helplessness

Co-dependency is different to Learned Helplessness. Learned Helplessness is a mental condition where people, through conditioning from another person/s (the perpetrator/s and the criminals as in the above case of the slaves), learn to survive the abuse and no longer try to live the life they deserve. These people (the victims) have been continuously told of their lack of ability, live with the fear of their family being hurt or killed or told '... you are stupid and incompetent and '...you will not achieve anything in your life...' With such conditioning, the victim loses the will and determination to do anything other than what they have been told they can do; they lose the will to challenge; they live in the state of Learned Helplessness.)

To help to fill their criminal behaviour, the criminals may also have drug related habits, have drug related connections, and use mind-altering substances.

What Is Stress?

Meichenbaum (1977) his assumption being: *'...stress is caused by faulty processing of information....'[11]*

There's more about Meichenbaum's theory in Chapter Eleven.

'Stress is a mental and emotional state creating apprehension and pressure in an individual through over- demanding circumstances.' (Thompson-Wells 2014)

---

[11] Meichenbaum, D (1977) Cognitive-behaviour modification

18

After reading the study of the Polish Slaves, ask yourself: *'How could I take a challenge and turn it into a winning solution?'*

If you cannot think at this time, read on, and come back to this page when you feel you are ready.

Note: As you read on, do not dismiss this page – come back to it from time-to-time and think it through until you can come up with an answer.

There is an answer waiting to be found!

When you start to work with your mind in this way, you will have a surge of positive *stress* that will assist you in your search.

Your Notes

....
....
....
....
....
....
....
....
....
....
....
....
....
....
....
....
....
....
....
....

Chapter Two

Your Precious Brain and Mind – Understanding how your brain and mind work

How we use our brain and mind will dictate how we live.

In the previous chapter, I have mentioned the 'brain gearbox'. It is strange to mention the gearbox of a motor vehicle when speaking about how our brains' work! It is, however, the simplest way of describing the brain and the treasure it holds. It is how we drive our brains that will allow us to live successful lives. Knowing to live a successful life is also to reduces stress.

Most people are born with the ability to make changes in their life, however, as we have seen in the previous chapter with the Polish slave story, some people are caught up in learned helplessness. Learned helplessness can be forced on people when:

1. They do not understand the language of the culture they are living within (As in the Polish Slave story)
2. Through fear, they are forced to live in subservient or enforced situations
3. Because of fear, (threats to family members and other loved ones), they are not given a reason or choice when asked to do or commit a crime or to make criminal acts of violence against another human being
4. They have no choice in what they do; it becomes part and the way they live
5. All reason and purpose for their life is taken from them
6. Because of the past cruelty they have experienced, they know no other existence.

Culture, ethnic background, attitudes of the family we join at birth, and many other factors can, but not always, contribute to the way we think and use our brain and mind.

As each person grows from childhood into adulthood there are many questions, we may ask of ourselves:

1. What is my existence all about?
2. Who am I?
3. What am I meant to be doing in this life?
4. I need to find the reason of why this or that has happened?
5. Why haven't I got direction in my life?
6. Why is my life so difficult?
7. Why was I born? and other significant questions, when we are indeed seeking or looking for answers and change.

The above are significant questions and often happen during adolescents. We do, however, *change* as maturity takes over. These changes can produce many stressful times in our lives.

To *change* for the better takes positive amounts of energy and that energy happens because, as a person, you are wanting direction in your life. When such significant questions as outlined in the above are asked by your mind and brain, there is a power of energy and movement taking place. That power and movement is created through the interaction of electrical waves sending messages to and from your sub-conscious and conscious mind held within your brain.

The story of our brain and its evolution is similar the world over. The human brain is the grey and white coloured organ that sits within the skull. The brain consists of three separate and dynamic areas that work for you. Please remember, the brain is made up of many electrical circuits that work within the glia (the grey and white substance in the brain.) Each part of the brain is a workhorse working inside your head to give you direction and answers. The answers come from the intricate connections of the electrical circuits which are part of the neuron pathways and the synapse sparks that happen when you are looking for solutions to problems and other questions you may be asking.

The first brain (or brain one) – the cerebellum

The cerebellum is thought to be the first part of the human brain to develop. This brain operates your gross and fine motor movements. Your gross motor movements allow you to drive your car, dig in the garden or load the bricks to build a house. The fine motor movements allow you to thread a piece of cotton through a small sewing needle opening; you can only do this with the help from the electrical communication through your neuron pathways that help to operate your muscular movement that send messages from your cerebellum. If the cerebellum is not working, your co-ordination, in the simple task of threading a needle, will be difficult to do.

The cerebellum, and the role it plays, has been underestimated for centuries or decades. This brain is also known as the small or reptilian brain. The cerebellum is immature at the time of your birth but develops over your childhood and is thought to mature through your teenage years and into your mid-twenties or – from fifteen to twenty-five. Its shape and structure resemble that found in the brains of reptiles; hence, this is why, it is called the reptilian brain. This old brain has collected information for its owners over millions of years.

The cerebellum brain is small by contrast to brains two and three, (in size, nothing more than a small-clenched fist). It sits tightly under the left and right upper hemispheres of your cerebral cortex.

The cerebellum is a complex mechanism that makes powerful connections to other parts of the brain and forms part of your *messaging service*. Your *messaging service* incorporates millions of connections made to and from neuron transmitters within your brain and body.

With incoming information and data from your senses, the cerebellum continually searches, looks for answers, seeking questions and sorting out stimuli. Stimuli are the collection of information, ideas or thoughts that come together in your mind when you are looking for answers to your questions.

To give you some idea: if you are walking into unforeseen danger, the information given back to you may come in the form of a feeling: the hairs on the back of your neck stand up or you may receive an internal message: *'don't go there; it's not right for you,'* or *'this is dangerous, don't do it!'* Internal messages may come from your subconscious mind!

With an incoming warning of *'...don't do it...'* the cerebellum is working with heightened *stress* levels which are interacting with your senses. Without this heightened *stress* level, you may not receive the warning message!

This *messaging service* is a system and like all systems needs to be kept clean and healthy to operate effectively. You can send messages to your consciousness within a nanosecond to protect and keep you safe.

These messages incorporate a combination of your past experiences, thoughts and ideas and your inherited instincts, which are footprints from your ancestors and given to you at birth; all of which are thought to be contained within your subconscious mind and are thought to exist in your cerebellum.

Your *messaging service* consists of a collection of highly developed neuron cells that work through your motor and sensory receptors. Your receptors work throughout your brain and body interacting continuously and work with your Emotional Intelligence.

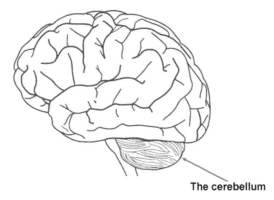

The cerebellum

The cerebellum sits at the lower part of your skull at the back of your head – now, touch the back, lower part of your head and feel the hollow – that's as close as you can get to touching your cerebellum.

Until recent years, little has been known about your different brains and the roles they play in your life.

It is important to get to know your cerebellum and the important and vital role it plays in your everyday living; it allows you to do the jobs you need to do in order to survive.

It is also important to understand that all parts of the brain deserve to be respected, loved, and nurtured.

Damage to the cerebellum

Ataxic Cerebral Palsy

'Hunter is a 20-year-old man. He has poor muscle coordination and struggles to make quick movements. He trembles when reaching for items. He has some depth perception and balance issues. His walk shows strange planting of the feet with an awkward distance between his legs. His intelligence is unaffected by his disability.

- *6% Cerebellum damage*
- *Characterized by shaky movements (tremors) when they make quick movements or movements that need a lot of control, like writing.*
- *Affects balance and sense of positioning in space/coordination.*
- *Problems with balance and coordination. They may be unsteady when they walk.*
- *This is the least common form of cerebral palsy.'[12]*

Many people experience road accidents, they may also experience trauma when the cerebellum is damaged.

---

[12] https://neurologycp.weebly.com/case-study.html

All wars produce victims of war. Many people suffer horrible injuries and once the war is over, they try to live a normal life.

Victoria

As a child, Victoria noticed her dad's continual shaking. It was not until after his death that she noted on his Death Certificate: Cerebellum damage. This answered a lot of questions for her.

Despite his brain injury and his condition, he always had work and provided a good home for his family.

It is only in recent years that we have become aware of the role of the cerebellum and its importance in the working and the co-ordination of our muscle movements.

These muscle movements allow us to iron the child's dress, sew on the button of a shirt or blouse, dry the crystal glass with care, sign a document and do the other jobs we continually take for granted.

The cerebellum, is indeed, a valuable part of you and a valuable companion that constantly works for you, and you, alone.

The cerebellum is part of your neuron *messaging service* that works for you 24/7.

Writing this book is only done because my cerebellum is working in unison with my mind as I operate the keys on the keyboard of the computer. I have past knowledge from the research I have done and draw on stories told to me. I then pass this information onto you through the pages in this book. All of this is done through the help from my *cerebellum!'*

When you are cold, you may put on another jumper or coat to make yourself warm. The message and the mix of information is being transferred to the working cerebellum would be: *'you are cold'* – solution: *'put on another coat to make yourself warm!'*

Equally, the outgoing messages may include other actions to take place such as, if you do not have a warm enough coat: *'buy one when you are next out shopping or if money is tight, ask a friend if they have a spare coat, or go to the second-hand shop to see if there are any coats for sale...'* The action you take will bring about the outcome of becoming warm!

As shown above, the cerebellum plays its role; it allows you to perform everyday tasks such as making yourself warm when you are cold, cooking a meal for the children, tying the laces of the child's shoe and further doing actions that allow you to peel vegetables, even putting on a pair of shoes and to tie the laces which allow the shoes to stay on your feet while you walk. All, of these skills are supported through your cerebellum working with you and for you.

To understand a little more about the *messaging service* and the messages sent to your mind, we need to discuss the role of the upper, outer two parts of the brain – the cerebral cortex: brains two and three.
You may ask at this point, why is she telling me so much about the brain when this book is about stress? The answer is simple, your brain operates how you react to stress and the way you work with your brain and mind to reduce stress.

Brain Two and Three

The cerebral cortex is where brain two and three sit inside your head, they are the upper part of the brain structure and are often referred to as the new brain. The new brain looks like the familiar shape often represented by the shelled appearance of the walnut half.

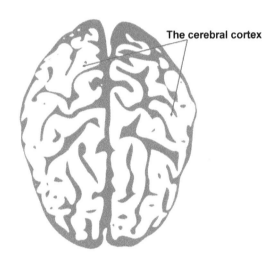

The cerebral cortex

The cerebral cortex sits within the left and right-hand side of the human skull and is divided by the corpus callosum; the corpus callosum allows information to be transferred from the left to right side of the cortex and vice versa. As I have said, both sides of the cerebral cortex resemble the appearance of a newly shelled walnut. The walnut, like the brain, is also divided into two halves!

The cerebral cortex is thought to have developed later in the evolution of the human species and therefore is often called the new brain. This brain, unlike the cerebellum, does sleep; it takes time out to rest, renew, and restore its energy. It takes in the information from your senses, sifts, sorts, stores, and passes it on to the cerebellum again, for filtering, sifting, sorting, and storing.

Relevant information is kept by the cerebellum, the worthwhile information is sent back to the cerebral cortex. Within the cerebral cortex there are many functions that allow you to live your daily life, one function includes your memory.

Two of the most important functions of the cerebral cortex are the use of your short and long-term memory. By using your short and long-term memory in conjunction with your cerebral cortex and your cerebellum, you have the ability to learn how to write, learn mathematics, and science formula, develop your spatial awareness so that you can do the tasks which include: drive on the road system, plumb a house, fly an aircraft, design a building, paint a room, make a child's dress – shave your face if you are a male, or apply your makeup if you are a female.

Your brain works with the interconnection of your *messaging service*, and with the help from your cerebellum, and cerebral cortex. These essential sections of your brain help to send electronic messages to your limbs and other parts of your body. It signals action to take place or happen and to the co-ordination of your muscle movement in your hands, legs, feet, and other parts of your body that allow you to function and live your life normally.

Your brains are working with every piece of received, incoming information. The way you interpret the incoming information will dictate the *stress* level you work with.

To give you some idea, if your senses are interfered with through accident, drug-taking or through other damage, the *messaging service* to your brains can also be interfered with. If this has happened to you, you know you may have to learn how to *learn new* skills. Once learnt, you will need to develop the new actions so that the skills become a part of you – all of such learning requires a form of heightened positive *stress*.

Having a basic awareness of how your *messaging service* works will allow you to continually learn and apply new skills whether damaged or not.

(Please Note: Some written or spoken information relates to the brain as the forebrain, the midbrain, and the hindbrain – each, within its own context, is correct.)

Information from your living environment travels from your senses and to your brains

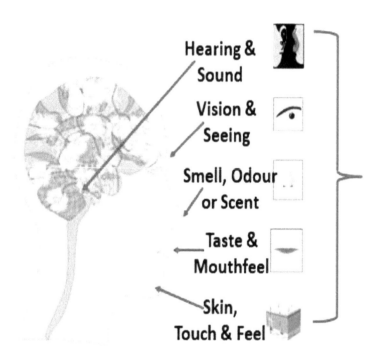

Hearing & Sound

Vision & Seeing

Smell, Odour or Scent

Taste & Mouthfeel

Skin, Touch & Feel

You have many, if not millions, of senses working within your human system. On this page, I am speaking about the easily identified senses; these are the gateways to your *messaging service*. Your senses are interconnected to your three brains and each brain works with the information it receives, processes it, and then passes it on to your mind.

The human mind

The human mind is made up of interacting, interconnecting, electrical circuits within the human brain. The human mind is not the human brain. It is the interaction of filtered information being processed within the cerebellum and cerebral cortex that formulates and makes the human mind work.

The human mind is a combination of interacting, interconnecting, electronic pathways within the human brain

These pathways connect at different times, through the different commands that you give it. Commands and connections are made and come from the different life experiences you have had from your home, and living environment, and from the culture and the family values you have been brought up with. The mind also incorporates your values and beliefs and your life philosophy.

Every time a piece of information is received from the senses, the brain and mind kick into action and uses the information which is the most appropriate for you – this becomes your filtered information.

Your filtered information is usually the information you take action on, such as: scratch your head if you have an itch, clean your teeth when you feel your mouth needs refreshing, wash or comb your hair, go to the hairdresser when you hair needs a cut, run for the bus if you need to catch that bus that will take you to the right stop in town and so on. Each of these actions contain either action and reaction, cause and effect or stimulus and response. These three actions are known as sensitivities and sensitivities are linked to your senses, thought, and the actions you take.

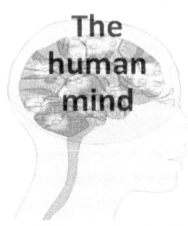

Each of the three sensitivities mentioned work in conjunction with your needs and wants.

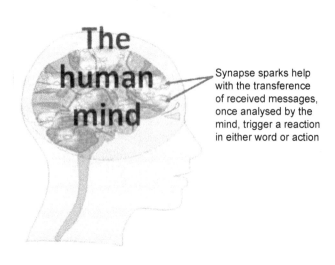

Synapse sparks help with the transference of received messages, once analysed by the mind, trigger a reaction in either word or action

When synapse fail to spark, normal communication does not take place. Two conditions that show these reactions are Alzheimer's disease, Huntington's disease, and like disorders.

Science is now proving that a synapse can fail to spark when they have aluminium deposits interfering with the transference of the spark. This interference also restricts the flow of filtered information. The filtered information is stored in your cerebral cortex and within the memory banks. This filtered information allows you to accumulate good, positive information or negative destructive information.

We can all be a victim of collecting destructive information and the storage of it. If you do not vigilantly look after the type of information you store, you will start to go down a negative and destructive pathway in life. By collecting negative information, you are adding to your negative stress.

The brain is often referred as the computer inside your head. However, the human brain is a grey and white heavy organ that sits within your skull. The physical weight of the brain is between (1360 grams or 3 pounds or 1.3 – 1.4kg). The collective three brains allow your human mind to operate.

To compare the human brain with that of a computer is to underestimate the power of the human brain and mind – it is after all, the human mind that created the computer in the first place…!

Without your three brains working at their best capacity, the mind struggles to work.

Your brains and mind need to work in unison, by doing this you initiate the voluntary muscular movements that will allow you to walk down the street, ride a bike, write a letter, do the washing up, hang out the washing, write a report and more movements.

The muscular movements of your body also include involuntary movement such as bowel movements and your heartbeat.

In order, for the body to function properly, stress need to be kept to a minimum or at least managed.

The incoming information and data may come from your body or your environment. If it comes from your body and for instance: you have a sore throat, your mind will compute, because of the possible past history of sore throats; it knows the signs of a virus or germ that is invading your throat and body. Intuitively, you know that something is wrong, and you are not well. When a person becomes sick, their body is under strain, and stress can accumulate in your body.

It is the same process for the incoming information from either your body, living environment home or work that works with different stressors you experience daily. All incoming information is processed in this way and comes from the information collected by your senses, it is your senses that alert you to the stress you are experiencing.

With a sore throat, you may have a runny nose and your eyes may be burning; you may have a sinus attack or something that is causing hay fever. You may not receive this vital information if your *messaging service* is not working properly!

The information from your senses is accumulated over your lifetime, and the more positive information that is added, the better equipped you are to cope with situations and life *challenges,* especially when you are looking for vital answers to troublesome questions!

Of course, there are instances, because of new incoming information, you cannot access an immediate answer to a problem or find a solution to a dilemma. If this is so, you will need to accumulate more information or data from your senses to allow you to form an opinion that will lead you to an answer. While you are looking for answers, you need some good positive *stress* to work with you!

Sometimes, because of the lack of incoming data or information, the answer is not ready when you need it! This can lead to frustration, annoyance, and stress – it can also lead to negative *stress* so you will need to become sensitive to your feelings.

Sometimes, you just have to wait for more incoming information to make a complete picture in your mind or wait for one last piece of the jigsaw puzzle to fit before you can form your opinion and take the next action. All, of the life processes we go through daily take different levels and types of stress. Each stress reaction has a title and is covered in Chapter Five.

Servants

I have spoken in this chapter about the three brains we each have sitting inside our heads. I have also touched on the human mind. When the brain and mind are sick or damaged, it becomes difficult for them to work. The brain and mind are also constant friends. They do not ask for payment, they ask to be looked after and shown respect.

Many brains are not respected, they are abused by their owners through the overuse of toxins in the form of drugs, alcohol, and other poisons. Once taken, whether orally or by injection, is released into the blood stream and then seep from the blood stream into the human brain and other organs and tissue (soft and otherwise) within the body.

Though, such tiny cells, the brain and mind are gifts we receive that grow and develop within twenty-one days after conception, and in size, is no more than a tiny hair. The brain and mind are the servants we each have within our heads; their sole purpose is to work for our wellbeing.

If people were educated into the value of these gifts, one has to ask, 'would they ever want to willingly destroy them through drug taking?'

The mind and brain do not like to be idle; they like to be productive and work and to feel the satisfaction of the work. There are many truths in the saying: *'An idle mind is a devil's playground!'*

When an individual is idle, they can become mischievous. The brain and the mind are the workhorses held within our heads. When a workhorse is not working it can become irritable, agitated, and counter-productive, and get you into trouble – thus trouble leads to many areas and levels of negative *stress*!

When you have experienced negative incoming information that is counter-productive to your wellbeing, it has come from your senses. You may have been in the wrong place at the wrong time, said the wrong thing at the wrong time, been with the wrong people at the wrong time or done the wrong thing at the wrong time!

There are times in our life when we may have the thoughts:

- 'Why did I do that?'
- 'I should have thought first before I did that!'

- 'I wish I had known that…!'
- 'If only I had this information before I did that…!'

And so, the lamentations continue.

If you are not familiar with how your brain and mind work, the lamentations you hold about past experiences may inadvertently store negative information Negative information, actions done or words spoken are stored in your mind in the same way as other incoming information. Negative information may also be buried and re-surface at inappropriate times causing you all sorts of problems!

Buried negative information will add to your accumulated stress and such stress can weigh heavily on your shoulders

Thought for the day!

If you have had an outcome from the previous 'Thought for the day' write it down. You are now alert – the solution is either found or on its way. Do not dwell on it, move on to the next *Challenge.*

....
....
....
....
....
....
....
....
....
....
....
....
....

When working in positive *stress* and as you face each concern and work with your mind, piece by piece, your mind looks for positive solutions.

```
┌─────────────────────────────────────────────────────┐
│           Small Concern – Write It Down               │
│                                                       │
│   Concern or Problem                                  │
│                                                       │
│   Solution 1                                          │
│                                                       │
│   ..................................................  │
│   ..................................................  │
│   ..................................................  │
│   ..................................................  │
│   ..................................................  │
│                                                       │
│   Solution 2                                          │
│                                                       │
│   ..................................................  │
│   ..................................................  │
│   ..................................................  │
│   ..................................................  │
│   ..................................................  │
│   ..................................................  │
│                                                       │
└─────────────────────────────────────────────────────┘
```

Please Note: I have introduced you to the Three Brain Theory in this chapter. As you read through the rest of the book, I will speak of the brains as *the brain* but you are now aware that there are three distinct and different areas of the brain which only work for you.

Getting to know how your brain and mind work are important. Please, if you have not done so, touch the back, lower part of your head and feel the hollow space at the base of the skull.

This hollow is where you locate your cerebellum.

Your thoughts, experiences, answers to your questions, solutions to your problems are being worked on 24/7 – that is every second, minute and hour of every day within your cerebellum.

Please take a break and think of at least one concern or problem you have and then try to think of two positive solutions that could help you – use your past experience and don't forget to ask for help from your mind.

If you do not ask for help from your mind – you will not find the answers you are seeking!

....

....

....

....

....

....

Your Notes

....
....
....
....
....
....
....
....
....
....
....
....
....
....
....
....
....
....
....
....

Chapter Three

Your Three Ego Personality States

Because we all have a brain, and each person has a mind, it is difficult to not include some of the same or similar information in the books I write, so please forgive me if I appear to repeat myself.

According to Dr Eric Berne author of, *The Games People Play* – Berne (1964)[13]   Berne identified three Ego Personality States: **Parent, Adult** and **Child**. Each one of these mind states plays a significant and different role within your personality and individuality.

Your personality includes your traits, these are your inherited characteristics which contain your values, behaviour, qualities, and your distinctiveness. Into this *mix* of personality there are the three Ego Personality States that Berne identified.

Berne's model: Parent, Adult and Child ego personality states

---

[13] Berne, Eric (1964) The Games People Play

Your Parent ego personality state

The Parent Ego Personality State can be domineering, overbearing, and demanding to the point of being dictatorial to other people. This state can be identified when a bully is taking control.

Your Adult ego personality state

As an adult in this state of being, you can use incoming information to make balanced judgements and decisions.

You also have three choice factors:

1. *Use the information to create a positive outcome (Adult Ego Personality State)*

2. *Do nothing with the information (Child or Parent Ego Personality State)*

3. *Misuse and abuse incoming information – create alternative situations which may be distorted, biased, contaminated or contrived and seen only from your Child or Parent Ego Personality State.*

The adult ego personality state is the preferred state to work within

Working with your Adult ego personality state allows you to see reason and logical purpose in what you say and do.

Your Child ego personality state

When you work with your Child ego personality state, you are coming from the same emotional base as a two or three-year-old child; it is a *child centric* state that has no reasoning and comes from the: *You want* and *You will* get and if you don't get your way, *You will stamp your feet until you get what you want!*

The Child ego personality state does not help you when you are supposed to be an adult and a mature person living in the adult world.

As an adult, you need to take incoming information into your Adult ego personality state, work with the information and then come up with a workable outcome leading to a positive solution. If you work from your Child ego personality state, a workable outcome is not going to be forthcoming. Your maturity level, while in the Child ego personality state, is not within your thinking.

With exceptions, the Child ego personality state can help you when you need to be creative in your working environment. Working with the Child, while working for an income is a controlled Child state. It is a state that is needed and is a healthy state when working with your artistic ability and talents.

You will also use your Child ego personality state when being creative and productive as in creative cookery, design, marketing, art, and other areas of your creative development.

When there's not an understanding of how the ego personalities work, even the most level-headed, intelligent, educated person can, at times, say the most ridiculous of things or make the most nonsense statement or do the most ludicrous of actions!

When you think of the different combinations of personality ego states that people work within, is it any wonder that we all scratch our heads, from time-to-time, in wonderment at the things we do and say?

Why the young can get into trouble or lose their way

'Delinquency is suggestive of the failure of parents and society to raise the child rather than the failure of the child. Left unattended, there is nothing more devastating for a society than a juvenile delinquent developing into a dangerous criminal with the coming of age.' [14]

Many young people get into trouble with the law and authorities. So many of these people have become disillusioned in their life and then commit crime, some are sorry for what they have done, and others are not.

With many young people, there is a disconnect to the world they live in and the world that the remainder of us live in. Having taught both in a young offenders' institution and a jail for adults, one thing is evident, many of these people do not have the basic education or background to allow them to live in the community as the community demands.

Science is discovering new contributions that our brains play in our existence. In recent years, the time it takes for the brain to mature and for the neuron connections to develop has been identified. Many young people do not have their complete neuron pathways in place until they are in their mid-twenties. This lack of neuron placement leaves the person exposed to making choices that they may not make when they are a little older. With this knowledge, and if a young person does not have the right guidance in their life, they can and do get into trouble or serious trouble.

---

[14] http://infomory.com

Together with the lack of neuron connections, mature guidance, and if they are on a poor diet containing sugar, processed food that contain many food additives, the young person and their behaviour can easily go out of control. My own research in my book, '**Devils In Our Food**' identifies many behavioural problems that can be linked to food additives.

Gottengen minipigs

Using measured sugar intake for twelve days, a study was conducted on Gottengen minipigs a particular breed of swine. The study revealed through PET imaging, that increased levels of dopamine, a hormone produced in the brain, was evident. Dopamine is a pleasure-seeking hormone that wants more of the drug, in this instance, sugar, once ingested. Sugar is an opioid and is addictive. Stimulating the 'Pleasure Centre' or (ventral tegmental area) of the brain in young people will change behaviour, usually showing itself in behavioural problems.

The authors of the study revealed: *"After just 12 days of sugar intake, we could see major changes in the brain's dopamine and opioid systems. In fact, the opioid system, which is that part of the brain's chemistry that is associated with well-being and pleasure, was already activated after the very first intake."*[15]

For decades, the intake of sugar has been debated. My own research has also pointed to sugar as an opioid stimulant on the brain. The conclusion of the study suggests *'...foods high in sucrose influence brain-reward circuitry in ways similar to those observed when addictive drugs are consumed.'*

---

[15] Michael Winterdahl Scientific Reports www.medicalnewstoday.com www.nature.com

Many young people end up in prisons and reform institutions when they have committed an offence or have out-of-control behaviour, questions need to be asked primarily about their intake of food and their food intake habit!

Behaviour and sugar or opioid intake

The intake of different foods can and does interfere with the brain and this interference is shown in the behaviour exhibited.

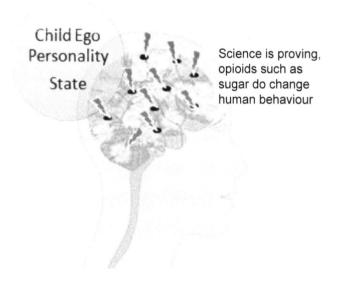

Child Ego Personality State

Science is proving, opioids such as sugar do change human behaviour

Young Offenders

I have spoken many times about my experience when teaching and counselling young offenders. What was apparent early on with my work was the poor-quality of food the young offenders were offered while they served their prison term. The food consisted of deep-fried, processed food with little green or fresh vegetables added to their diet. To add taste appeal, many food manufacturers add sugar and other poisons. Such food does not help the young developing brain. In fact, current research shows these foods can bring on, not only behavioural problems but assist with premature blindness and deafness.

Frightening facts

'Recently released in The Telegraph, United Kingdom was an article on a boy who only ate white bread, crisps, chips and processed meat for about a decade. The seventeen-year-old, after eating this diet has now been classed as legally blind and deaf.[16]

Bad eating habits need to be broken early and before the child has the mental time to establish them.' Extract from my book: **'Devils In Our Food.'**

Please Note:

The Child ego personality state: Not all adults, have the ability, to do *spot checks* on where their Child ego personality state is coming from. In some instances, sufferers with Asperger syndrome may stay locked into their Child ego personality state for their life duration.

Asperger syndrome is a form of autism and a condition where the sufferer has limited but obsessive interests and may have difficulty relating, with empathy, to other people. People who suffer such mental conditions may have difficulties relating to their Adult ego personality state.

---

[16] Dominic Lipinski/PA Lizzie Roberts, The Telegraph UK 3/9/2019

Can you recall a time when you went into your Child ego personality state and took over, and you did not know why? This personality can be seen when people are under stress; their mind might be racing, and they have accumulated worries.

The Reality Is –
You can only live with the current or *NOW* time.

To make your life manageable, list four actions you can take or do NOW or Today.

Action 1

....

....

Action 2

....

....

Action 3

....

....

Action 4

....

....

Sometimes life is difficult to cope with; to be successful and have a life that is going to add benefits to everyday living – stress and life must be managed.

10 Tips to manage life and stress

1. Deep breathing

My research and my own experiences have shown me that breathing deeply is the key to managing stress. Many people only use 1/3rd of their lung capacity when they breathe. Their breathing is shallow, and their blood is not receiving the oxygen it needs to receive to keep them either stress-free or with managed stress. Fresh oxygen is passed from the lungs and into the blood. Fresh oxygen allows you to maintain your health, to have the energy required to meet each new challenge of each new day.

2. Exercise

Daily exercise is important for the body and mind. Doing regular exercise will allow you the time to think, make plans and to work positively towards your future. Doing regular exercise also helps you to intake the new fresh oxygen so desperately needed by your body, and brain.

3. Relaxation

Learning to relax, after possibly many years of tension in your life, it may not be as easy as it sounds. Many people have developed life changing habits such a cigarette smoking and drug taking, even drinking too much caffeine can cause stress to the body and brain. Drinking too much caffeine can disguise the stress in your body and brain.

Healthy eating

The offender to many health issues is the junk food revolution and junk food industry. Junk food is eaten by many thousands of people daily, and throughout the world. This pandemic of eating habits has caused more health issues and future health issues, still not seen, in people globally. There is evidence that many foods contain aluminium. Aluminium is contained in many toothpaste products, breads and dough products, and other widely eaten foods globally. Please see my book, **Devils In Our Food** for more information. Foods containing any synthetic or unnatural additives add stress to the body and brain.

4. Living with the moments

We often think of the days and hours we have to do a job but what we don't think about are the moments that make up the minutes, hours and days and indeed the years we have in life. Each minute, hour, day and year are made up of moments and each moment our brain and body are working for us. It is using each moment appropriately that will help you to manage negative stress while managing moments help you to achieve your goals and dreams.

5. Time-out

Giving yourself permission to take time-out from the demands of everyday life is permissible. Catching trains, running for the bus for work are demands on your body and mind. Preparing the food for regular meals under time constraints, doing the washing and ironing so it is ready for school on Monday, and other time-demanding chores are exhausting. Students in study also need to take permissible time-out. As a writer, I too, need to give myself permissible time-out. I do this by taking time-out to do physical and breathing exercises. I like to use this time constructively and to reach my goal of working with my body and mind. These activities allow me to think clearly and to work with the words on the screen.

I have mentioned this experience in some of my books and I recall the time I went down to our local church for a Sunday service. The Rector's wife spoke about the 'Niches in Time'. From that time until now, I work in the 'Niches in Time, and it is remarkable by using this method of 'Time-Out' how effective it is.

6. Developing hobbies

How important it is to connect to the soil? Gardening is good for, not only reducing stress, but for exercise, brain and body health and health of the senses. The colours of the flowers and foliage in springtime can become addictive to the eyes, they just want to see more as different colours and textures emerge. Some people find that Train Spotting is enjoyable, others, use sport or car racing as a hobby. When I have time, I love to paint large flower paintings. Developing a hobby is a personal choice, it warms the heart, adds the 'feel-good' feelings we all need to keep us mentally healthy and reducing stress.

7. Problems – a problem has a solution waiting to be found

Problems are those situations that have a solution, but the solution can sometimes take time to find. When we have a problem, and stress, and accumulated stress, the problem can become larger than it is. Our clever brain, when it is combined with our mind, can often present the solution. However, with stress, the solution can become elusive. By doing the steps, or some of the steps above, solutions to problems can be forthcoming. Please remember, your brain and mind are obedient servants. If you are thinking of destructive solutions to problems, you will accumulate destructive actions and stress, this then becomes revenge or 'get-even and this is not the purpose of this book.

Problems need to be spoken about before the problem becomes too large in your thinking. If you are feeling this is happening to you, please seek professional support. The moment you reach out and speak about your problems, you will instantly start to feel better and you will reduce the stress you are carrying in your body and mind.

8. Do not beat yourself up

Does it come as a surprise, when you punish yourself for something you have done either recently or in your distant past, and you are still punishing yourself for the actions you have taken or the words you have spoken, you are indeed increasing your negative stress levels?

You have the ability, to forgive yourself for either the actions or words spoken that may have hurt another person. I have, on a number of occasions, some not in the immediate time, but some of the actions taken or words I have spoken and when I have realised, that was hurtful to another, said in sincere prayer and asked for forgiveness. I usually do this in my own quiet time. You will never be able to eliminate the memory from your mind, but you can lessen the pain of the memory. By saying you are sorry in either prayer or through your breathing exercises, the grip the memory has on your conscious mind is lessened, or released, therefore, the impact of negative stress is also decreased. Decreasing your stress levels allows you to grow and to do the important work or things you want to do in your life.

If you have the ability to speak to the person you think you may have hurt, and if you can speak to them in person, it can bring about a whole new beginning in your friendship.

9. All stress has a beginning

Stress, like other situations in our lives, has a beginning. If left unattended, stress will only get worse. Learning to manage your stress is your responsibility. From being a student, farmer, factory hand, millionaire, baker, or teacher, we each need to know how to manage stress. Managing stress is part of working with the Adult ego personality state.

10. The Adult ego personality state

In this chapter, I have spoken of the ego states. Getting into the inside of your head is getting to know about you and how you work in the different areas of your life.

Working with your Adult ego personality state increases your health and wellbeing. It allows you to take the responsibility for the actions you do, and the words you say. If saying sorry or apologising for something that has happened in the past is difficult for you to do, and you were in the wrong, you will need to grow into your Adult ego personality state. By growing into this state, you will become mentally stronger, reduce your stress, and prolong your longevity.

The power of your Adult ego personality state

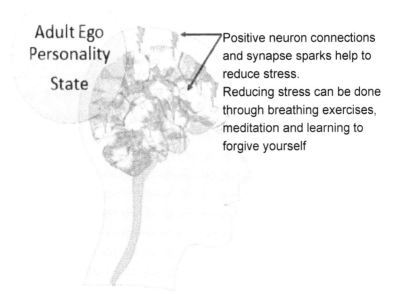

Adult Ego Personality State

Positive neuron connections and synapse sparks help to reduce stress.
Reducing stress can be done through breathing exercises, meditation and learning to forgive yourself

Please study the above image and think about how your personality states work in your brain and the ask yourself, *'how can I achieve the life I want by working this way?*

It is now time to take some time out to reflect on the last chapter, how can you use this information to reduce the stress you are experiencing?

Remember, your brain and mind have all the answers you are looking for, it is only with care and love for yourself that you will start to eliminate the stress you feel and the answers you want.

With the time you have taken out, write down below the thoughts that come into your mind. Do not punish yourself because of the thoughts you have. If they are negative, send it on its way with love. If the negative thought tries to invade your thinking, do not accept that thought.

....

....

....

....

....

....

....

....

Your Notes

....
....
....
....
....
....
....
....
....
....
....
....
....
....
....
....
....
....
....
....

Chapter Four

The Start – Your Ego Personality States, Emotional Intelligence and Your Inherited Instincts and Their Importance in Everyday Life and Role Confusion

Emotional intelligence has a way of getting people excited. People generally, want to know how they work inside their heads. The brain, and more so the mind, have mesmerised people for generations. Like so many areas of human thinking and action together with the ego personality states – emotional intelligence is an area of great interest which include:

- Employers to educators
- To people serving jail sentences
- Doctors and medical practitioners
- Architects designing interesting buildings that are different
- The business owner running a small business and competing with his or her competitors
- The student learning about fashion design and the latest colours for the season
- The teachers teaching psychology and other related topics and to
- The people who are victims of violence and the
- Victims of the Covid pandemic and their personal survival of the disease.

By all of the above, emotional intelligence is there, playing its role in every action taken and word spoken, and by all people throughout the world. Daily we work with and use emotional intelligence to help us through each day.

So, what is emotional intelligence?

I have been the Head of a Psychology Department at large girls' school in Berkshire in the United Kingdom. Since my own studies at university, I have been interested in the subject of human behaviour which is the study of Psychology.

Emotional intelligence is within the repertoire of the subject of psychology.

Research into emotional intelligence is ongoing in the schools, colleges, and universities in the United Kingdom. There are some researchers who conclude that '... *a high emotional intelligence score is more important than attaining a high IQ score ...!*'

If this is so, and simply put: the higher a person's emotional intelligence, the greater the chance of that person having success in their life.

Further research: young adults from the ages of eleven to sixteen show that a higher emotional intelligence has an impact on social behaviour.

The students who were studied and who work with their higher emotional intelligence in their behaviour: '... *take more responsibility for their behaviours and acceptance of the outcome if they have done something wrong!*'

The personal acceptance of doing something wrong shows maturity. These students also identified they were working from their Adult ego personality state.

Emotional intelligence and the Adult ego personality state

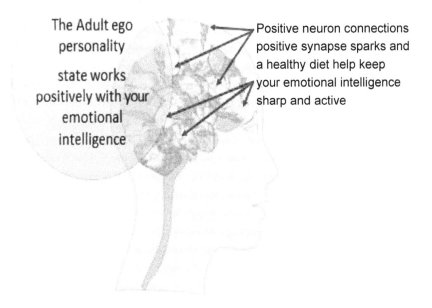

The Adult ego personality state works positively with your emotional intelligence

Positive neuron connections positive synapse sparks and a healthy diet help keep your emotional intelligence sharp and active

Lower scoring students working with their emotional intelligence may work from their Child ego personality state. Working from this state, when committing offences, allows the perpetrator to act or speak from a state of denial – there is little to no responsibility taken for the negative outcomes or actions they commit.

Maturation

Working with low maturation levels or working from the Child ego personality state was identified on the previous pages. So, what is maturation?

Maturation is a process of human development from child to juvenile and into adulthood. The modern concept of maturation includes the process of learning to cope with life and with appropriate behaviour. Maturation also includes individual growth and development. Arnold Gesell 1940 identified nature's role, Jean Piaget identified, *'A child cannot undertake certain tasks until they are psychologically mature enough...'*

The current thinking includes, (cognitive theory), maturation is a process of interaction between personal genetics, and the social environment the induvial lives within.

When you become aware of your emotional intelligence and the role your ego personality states play in everyday life, you will show respect for yourself and others, and work with each part of your personality appropriately. By doing this, you can become empowered to live the life you choose to live.

Getting to know your emotional intelligence and creating the ability of continually work with each ego personality state is an exciting, positive journey and the journey lasts as long, as you live. The added advantage of knowing how to work with your ego personality states and emotional intelligence is a positive way to work with controlling your *stress* levels – by this understanding alone, you are in the driving seat of your mind.

Role confusion

We live in the world of social media. Many people look to celebrities as their role models and adopt, what they think, is the latest model. By doing this, many people become 'stuck' not with their own identity, but with the identity of an adopted role model. I think most of us at some time, (it may be a limited time only…!) have wanted to be or to look like another person. If we look at David Beckham and his endorsement of tattoos by having visible tattoos inked over his body and now look at the number of people with tattoos, the world over, the numbers are high. Tattoos make a person look different, they are a form of identity, they are indeed a uniform to be worn. The fashion and a worldwide industry of inking can be traced back to celebrities and other famous people who wear tattoos.

All popular fashion and fads work in this way. Popularising a particular fad or idea can make people wealthy. It is an emotional 'must have'.

Many people may become caught up in role confusion. Though as fully grown adults, and throughout their life they may identify with their 'role model'. This could be labelled as 'Pop Culture'. It may also identify with the person working from their Child ego personality state. Working with this state is not necessarily a negative response as with working with hobbies, but it would need to be identified by the owner as part of their behavioural pattern.

And so, in all human actions or behaviours we work continuously with our three ego personality states. Each state works with and through the connection of each person's emotional intelligence –

the connection is made to and with the people we work with, live with, sell or trade to, or communicate with.

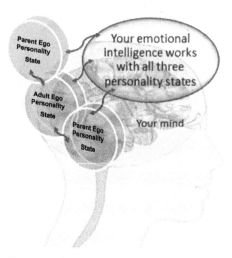

All people, in all countries, in all communities around the world regardless of faith, culture or birth right, work and live with, use their emotional intelligence 24/7.

When you have an understanding, of emotional intelligence, the game of life can become exciting and challenging.

You no longer see the negative outcomes you experience from the victim view point; you see the outcome as a *challenge* and a hurdle to overcome – the game of life is far too short to let a negative outcome take over!

When you understand this concept, you will automatically reduce your stress levels and see the value of all life experiences – whether, at the time, they are negative or positive!

71

Emotional intelligence may be seen, as an elusive butterfly, but it is not elusive, it is there working inside your head 24/7.

As I have said, this one subject alone causes excitement because we all want to know outcomes! Whether the outcome is the knowledge of your exam result, will he or she meet me in a week's time, or knowing how your emotional intelligence is going to rate when you fill in the questionnaire from a dating agency, or job application! Yes, this is all emotional intelligence. From knowing how you will manage in a Covid pandemic, if you will have a job in the future, what the kids are doing down in the back garden, to the counsellor counselling abused victims – simply said, everybody, without exception, uses emotional intelligence most of the time or all of the time in their life.

Working with your inherited instincts

Each person has a life code. It may include:

- Values
- Beliefs
- Individual or group philosophy
- Ideas and other significant and strongly accepted ways of living.

Through times of great worry, as with so many people worldwide, nobody knows what the outcome of the Covid pandemic will be. The questions we are all asking: 'Will there be a vaccine found?' This is a worrying situation for all people, worldwide.

We all hope, that one day, this question will be answered with a positive 'Yes' however, at this point, we still do not know!

In time of great worry, we need to work positively with our inherited instincts, these instincts provide us with survival powers. Our inherited instincts work with our emotional intelligence and the three personality states. Each of these mentioned are gifts that allow us to survive ordeals.

Working with your three ego personality states, emotional intelligence, and your inherited instincts.

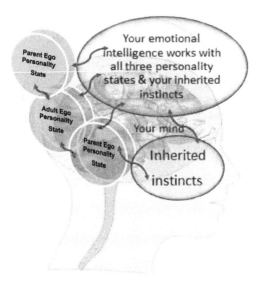

Each of the above work within your head. Inherited instincts are those parts of your personality which form part of your DNA.[17] Having said the above. People can be influenced through the different cultures they live within or through indoctrination to form other and different beliefs.

---

[17] DNA = Deoxyribonucleic acid is a molecule comprising of two polynucleotide chains which coil around each other to form a double helix. This double helix coil carries genetic instruction for the development and growth of reproduction of all organisms, including viruses.

Radicalisation, terrorism, and criminal activities

The above – radicalisation, terrorism and criminal activities exist because of a personal ideal, through indoctrination or through the desire to have power or personal gain. The above works from the emotional intelligence of each individual and an *Attachment* which people can identify with. Emotional *attachment* together with working with the Child emotional state within this form of human-bonding incorporates commitment to personal contracts.

Personal contracts and terrorism

Personal contracts are powerful mental tools and need to be managed with care. The role of the contract has an objective – the objective being, in this instance, to create terror both through the actions of the terrorist and to cast fear into the minds of other people. Without the bond between terrorists and the mental connection to other terrorists' emotional intelligence – terrorism would not exist.

Terrorism, it is suggested, is not a political call but rather the identity of one person to another seeking and identifying within a type of social solidarity; this solidarity forms a base of power. The base of power made by a terrorist leader is only made achievable by forcing a fear factor into the minds of other people or the victims unfortunate enough to be within the environment of the terrorist.

The mind of the terrorist comes from the Child ego personality state. Terrorism, like many criminal acts, is a type of sinister game that is further encouraged by strong bonding and the Child ego personality states of other terrorists, or criminals, who are committed to the same cause.

The emotional intelligence appears to be low of individual terrorists and criminals, and, yet research has revealed that some terrorists are extremely intelligent people. Because an individual terrorist may be intelligent, it does not mean they are mature adults working from their Adult ego personality state!

Terrorism, like so many criminal activities, does however start as a sinister *mind-game* and gains momentum when other players become committed to and take part in the game.

Terrorism, and long-term criminal activities, are games played that are almost irreversible to the individual or individuals, once there is a commitment to the game and is within their mind and mental contract!

More about role confusion

As people grow from being a child to adult, many people get caught up in a mind-state identified as *role confusion.*

Confusion of our roles in society can come about by being told one thing and its meaning being something different to what is being interpreted or encoded by the listener.

Encoding is the way we take a piece of information and interpret it, then use the interpretation to make a meaning which allows us to understand the incoming information.

Each person may experience, at different times in their life, when role confusion takes place.

- In relationships – a person may be in love with another, but the role may not be reciprocated
- In the workplace – the role you have is not clarified clearly or identified
- Within different friendships or family relationships
- Siblings rivalry and different parent attention
- Within research establishments
- Within government roles or diplomatic roles and many other roles, that we as an individual, carry out.

Role confusion is, and can be, part of the terrorist mindset and yet, role confusion can equally be part of what many people go through as they daily struggle to find their *own unique identity!*

In every home throughout the world, each, and every parent or carer, and family have different meanings for different words spoken, facial expressions made, and actions taken.

Different interpretations are put into place at different times, under different conditions and through different life experiences. What is accepted through the actions taken or words spoken in one home, one workplace or environment may not be accepted in another!

Thought for the day!

Can you identify a time in your life where you have experienced role confusion? Now that you have a brief description of role confusion, how do you think this understanding could help you in the future and did you notice your *stress* levels while in this state? Write your comments down.

....

....

....

Different cultures of the world

Moving from one country to another can be threatening and extremely *stressful* to individual's and their families.

Different word meanings and interpretations of spoken words can lead to individual hurt and pain. The person or people, as they try to adapt to their new living environment, and lifestyle, may struggle with the experience of misunderstanding, which then adds to the grief and stress of the experience in re-establishing their life.

The misunderstood interpretation may not be understood or possibly accepted by the people living and working within the already established community.

Like so many parts of the world, Australia is learning to adapt to different cultures who come to live in the country.

I too, came to live in Australia in the late 60s. My parents, brother and sister came to Australia in 1967. My parents were in the 40s when they arrived, and I know they struggled with adapting to their new living environment.

As I look back, I can now reflect and see the stress and the experiences they both experienced. These loving people, and the changes they wanted in their lives drove them on. Little did they know at the time, they were working with their Adult ego personality states to make the changes they made. Like so many migrants, they wanted a better life for their children.

I now think how brave they were to make a move to the other side of the world. But I also look now, having had that experience of my own parents, at the brave people who have newly arrived and some from war-torn countries. Many people adapt very well, while others struggle!

By observing my own parents and now with reflection, it has shown me that with positive determination, by working from a place of compassion, and from the Adult ego personality state, great changes can be brought about and into people's lives.

By working with your own emotional intelligence, you too, can make positive changes in your life. By acknowledging your brain, yes, it is there sitting inside your head, this servant is waiting to work with you. By giving some of your valuable time to think about your personality ego states and understanding how emotional intelligence, your inherited instincts, and your Adult ego state can work for you; his knowledge can add great advantages to people's lives.

Sub-cultures

Emotional intelligence can be interpreted very differently when used in different cultures. Within each culture, there are sub-cultures, these sub- cultures exist in our communities and exist in families, groups of people with a common interest such as horse riding groups, parent and teacher associations, church groups, painting and portrait artists, friends of art galleries, friends of the environment and so on.

A sub-culture is a cultural group existing within a larger culture but may have different values, philosophy, ideals, habits and possibly lifestyle to the larger population or group.

Role confusion – how did you cope?

Please identify a time you experienced role confusion and please think back and ask yourself, how did I cope?

Life Challenges!

Role confusion 1

....

....

Role confusion 2

....

....

Role confusion – how did you cope?

....

....

....

....

....

....

....

Each person experiences different life changes, you may have also experienced role confusion.

Some people experience more life changes and challenges than others – life has its *challenges*!

Think of a time when you were *challenged* and experienced *Role confusion*. You may have tried to mentally 'fill in the gaps' and tried to make yourself *fit into a situation, relationship or partnership that did not fit your life's role.*

Take time to think through your life and your experiences and ask yourself:

1) *'Did I experience role confusion over that time and*
2) *Did I find the experience stressful?'*

Your Notes

………………………………………………………………………………………

………………………………………………………………………………………

………………………………………………………………………………………

When you think about your past experiences, can you now see they were times of personal growth and those experiences have made you the person you are today? If the experience was tough and you still have problems trying to release the experience, try to let the memory go and work with your breathing to maintain a less stressful memory. More about relaxation later in the book.

There is more about breathing later in the book.

Your Notes

....
....
....
....
....
....
....
....
....
....
....
....
....
....
....
....
....
....
....
....
....

Unmanaged stress is a time bomb waiting to explode!

Chapter Five

Identifying Stress!

Briefly, there are seven areas of stress:

1. **Positive stress** allows you to get the job done
2. **Negative Stress** is destructive to your mind and body and needs to be controlled
3. **Transitional Stress** allows you to go from one situation, action, or spoken word to another.
4. **Accumulated Negative Stress** is stress you have experienced over a long period of time
5. **Post-traumatic Stress Disorder** (PTSD). PTSD can occur after experiencing or witnessing a major trauma
6. **Acute Stress** is the experience and the feeling of a lack of reality, life is just an existence!
7. **Hypertension** is high blood pressure.

As you read through the book, I will expand on stress.

In Chapter Four, I briefly spoke about emotional intelligence and how it plays different roles in your life.

Charles Darwin identified the importance of *'emotional expression'* (Emotional Intelligence) in the 1800s.

Your emotional intelligence is linked to your cognitive characteristics held within your mind and contributes to your memory and problem-solving abilities.

Using your cognitive ability allows you to learn, analyse, and make assumptions, and choices, thus, allowing thinking, learning, and understanding to take place.

The subject of emotional intelligence is buzzing in the twenty-first century. People appear to want to know more about the subject and how they can use the mechanisms within their emotional intelligence to better their lives and to live the life they want and choose to live.

From Darwin's theory in the 1800s to Thorndike's research, on the subject of, social intelligence, in the 1920s – the subject is within the realms of psychology and other contributing areas of human behaviour.

Howard Gardner's work held within his book *Frames of Mind*, introduced the idea of Multiple Intelligence in 1983.

Daniel Goleman's book in 2000, added to the theory of emotional intelligence by introducing, *'traits and ability...'* – a trait being a characteristic, inherited or otherwise, of the person. A trait also includes your talent or talents and contains the *ability to do the things you once thought you could not do!*

When you start to work with your emotional intelligence and can identify which ego personality state you are working within, a whole new insight comes into your life.

Because you are now thinking and working on another level of your intelligence, life starts to change – in most instances, for the better. I say this because multiple intelligences can be used for good or evil outcomes. If you remember, you have a very obedient mind, and it will always do what you give it instruction and permission to do. Therefore, there is a large responsibility on your part to work positively with your mind to achieve the best outcome for yourself, your family, and your community.

Assumption – the danger of assumptions

Throughout human history, assumptions have been made about human beings, human actions, re-actions, words said or acted upon, and the outcome of an assumption or assumptions. Assumptions can be dangerous when another person is the victim of an assumption. Assumptions may have little to no factual background and an assumption may belong with the *'gossip monger'*. Assumptions can fill your head and take up valuable memory space in your brain; it is wise not to get caught up in the 'assumption scenario'. People have been burnt at the stake, stoned to death, belittled, and ostracized because of a so-called assumption!

Often reflected in the work we do are the roles we play in life. Some of the roles played out are built on assumptions. When situations are taken out of context and assumptions are made, which have little to no factual foundation attached, it can lead to negative outcomes and loss to either you, your family, workplace, organisation or indeed, your future.

The assumption – when is it a fact or an assumption?

It was a busy afternoon in the school's art department and the class had worked hard. Mr White was happy with his students' work. Robert was an exceptional student with his talent. Mr White asked Robert to go to the Headmaster's office to show him the latest painting created over the last two weeks.

Once knocking on the Headmaster's door, Robert waited a while, eventually the door opened, the Headmaster invited Robert into his office. Unfortunately, Robert did not get to show the Headmaster his latest painting!

The Headmaster assumed that Robert had been sent to his office to have the cane. Robert received the cane and was sent back to his class. The Headmaster took no notice of Robert's painting or artwork!

This story emerged over forty years later when I met up with my school friends at a reunion in the United Kingdom.

Robert, now a Professor of Art at one of the British leading Art Schools, spoke about his ordeal on the night of our reunion. Robert, thankfully, did not let the caning stop him from pursuing his career.

Here, is seen how assumptions can be made; an innocent student was punished because of a negative assumption by the Headmaster.

Most adults have experienced a situation where they have been wrongly judged or a perceived judgement is passed without due consideration. Each, and every day, we all experience receiving thousands, if not millions, of messages. Some messages are non-verbal as in facial expression, hand and eye movements, verbal utterances, and leading or misleading cues! Some received messages are positive and some are negative!

Not all messages, at the time of being received, get the priority and attention or understanding required. Many negative messages can leave a person in a severe state of shock and stress. This may lead to a person losing their drive and determination – please do not let that be you. If you are in doubt, please, re-read Robert's story.

Wrong assumption – Robert – role confusion

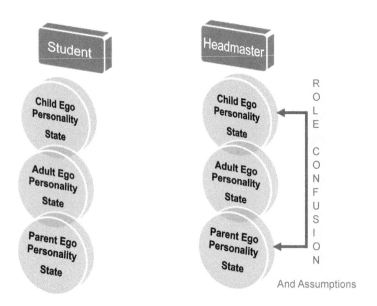

The model above shows how the mind can be changed through pre-conceived ideas, lack of knowledge and a wrong assumption.

There, maybe, a number of different issues, that take place within another person's life or environment – it is usually in busy or *stressful* times, that we experience unjust accusation or hurts.

The Headmaster and student study on the previous pages show how wrong assumptions take place. Wrong assumptions can and do take place many millions of times a day and in many environments around the world. All wrong assumptions lead to stress within the victim.

Conflict comes about, not only from assumptions, but by misunderstandings, different human needs, and wants and the lack of understanding to the recognition of emotional intelligence which is within itself – a human driver!

It is when, the interaction of the ego personality states become confused, the messages being sent from one person to another, that misunderstanding may take place!

Such misunderstandings may happen within families, executives in business negotiations or meetings, politicians creating policy, in teaching situations with teachers, young people in peer groups, parents, justice and judicial areas, work related environments, with and during diplomatic discussion, even neighbours living next door experience role confusion and make assumptions all of which lead to misunderstood messaging!

Misunderstood information leads to personal damage, damage to other people, belongings and to the environment, civil war, and wars.

Through education and learning, we can learn to understand how some of the mechanisms of the human mind operate. Of course, we cannot get inside another person's head, but understanding some of the outcomes of behaviour will at least allow us to function in a co-existing world. The paramount objective of this book is to understand how stress works, and once that is understood, how to manage the stress we each daily endure.

In a professional work environment, people need to work from the Adult ego personality state; this state allows effective communication to take place and creates a positive, effective, and workable, work environments.

From Headteachers, to construction workers in the Building Industry, the baker baking the daily bread, politicians, and the itinerant worker picking strawberries and vegetables for a living, each and every person needs to understand the meanings behind the message. If this does not happen, it leads to dissatisfaction, anger, embarrassment, and frustration of the victim.

Also built into the above is the value of respect.

Often, an authoritarian Parent ego personality state, which can become the aggressor, is the leftover residue from childhood. It is also the use of an *artificial powerbase* that goes to nothing once the victim has withdrawn from the situation.

The type of *perceived power* exhibited by the Headmaster, has little to no substance, however, it is still, many years later, within Robert's thinking.

There are many stories like Robert's. These stories can happen and do happen in many work settings and work environments. These incidents cause industry unrest, create strikes, and can become vengeful and counter-productive in any industry or organisation. Furthermore, civil unrest may be caused by people not understanding the role they are playing and the ego personality state they are working from.

Becoming aware of your emotional intelligence allows you to understand the roles you are working within; understanding allows you to switch mental gears. You can work in any of the: Parent, Adult or Child ego personality state gears – you are the one in the driving seat of your mind! This exciting new area of the human mind is discussed a little in this book and further in my next book: *How to Reduce Anxiety.*

Being aware of your emotional intelligence and how you can operate in the Parent, Adult or Child ego personality state, will allow you to gauge and take the appropriate action for each situation you find yourself in.

We each react differently to situations and events at different times in our lives!

Stress and difficult life situations

When you experience difficult and different life situations and have the feeling: *'I'm not coping with this situation – I feel stressed-out with this pressure.'* The stress and pressure you may experience may relate to everyday living you are:

- Trying to cope with the Covid pandemic and your reducing income.
- Experiencing sickness of yourself or a close family member.
- Your business is under threat.
- You are continually overworked, trying to *'make ends meet!'*
- You are concerned about older relatives and their health
- You are experiencing separation or divorce.
- You feel you have been unfairly treated and wrongly accused of something when you were doing your job.
- You have a dispute with your neighbour over noise, garden hedges, plants, and other issues!

And so, the number of stressors accumulate in your mind and body. Within each different, difficult, or changing event you encounter, you experience *transitional stress, in some instances you may go into accumulated stress!*

Accumulated stress is worry by magnitude and is a totally alien condition for your body and mind to experience.

Stress

Stress or stressors interfere with your:

- Health
- Home
- Work and
- Love relationships.

We are hard-wired to be survivors

We are not mentally wired to give in; that is the reason, the human species has survived until now. Without this mechanism of wiring, the human-race would have given up at the first hurdle, but we are still endeavouring to conquer and to reach out into the solar system, find solutions to disease and illness and to venture into how the human mind works.

Some of the different mechanisms inside your head – talking about stress

Please view to below model and come back to it when needed.

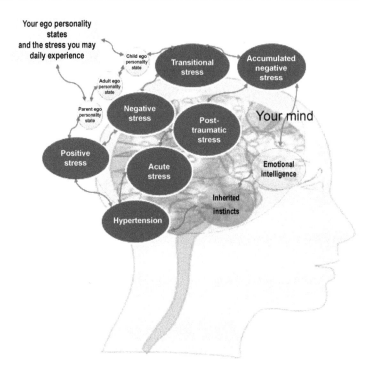

Stress is a mysterious subject because one single thought or job can take you into stress or the thought may stimulate a stressor[18].

Taking each stress separately

Positive stress not only allows you to 'get the job done' but also allows you to see, the finished job in your mind, before the job is completed. Positive stress is when you have a goal and 'by-hook-or-by-crook' you are going to complete that job. The job can be big as in building a house or starting up a new business, finishing high school studies, presenting your thesis after years of study and research, and many other big goals. Positive stress can relate to doing the large pile of ironing sitting in the laundry and waiting for your to do – regardless of any events, you get the job done.

Negative stress is the out of control situation where you allow worry to dominate your everyday living and work situation. Negative Stress is destructive to your mind and body and needs to be controlled

Transitional Stress allows you to go from one situation, action, or spoken word to another. It allows to have a flexible approach to your work and living conditions. You can manage many situations at one time. Because of this flexibility, your mind states are managed, and you possibly work from your Adult ego personality more often than you realise. This is an ideal state of mind to work within.

---

[18] A stressor or stimulus or threat that causes you to feel threatened through the thought of illness, examination, divorce, death of a loved one, loss of your job, moving-house, money worries and other threatening thoughts.

When a person has experienced trauma as in domestic violence, war, and other stressful times in their life, to be able to work within transitional stress is a positive step. If you have had difficult times, try to work with your mind from the Adult ego personality state and try to reach transitional stress. It may be difficult at first, but it is worth the work. While working in transitional stress, it allows you to take many positive steps. When stress types are identified, life can become easier to manage and you will be surprised at what you achieve.

If you need to, look at the image below and keep it in mind while you practise this exercise.

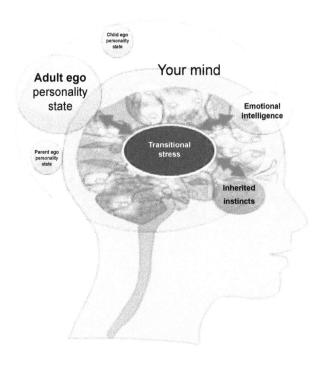

At first, you may find, you will need to work hard to keep this image in your mind, but it will become easier as time goes on.

a. Take the time out to think of the image and then try to go inside your head. While doing this, try to keep all negative thoughts out of your thinking.
b. Close your eyes and think of the image. Let go of the pain you may be experiencing and just think of the image, the image is you inside your head. Continue to do this little exercise every time you feel stressed. You can replace this image with a flower, country scene, tranquil water image or the image of a loved one. Try to keep your image positive. If you are grieving, the image of a passed loved one may add to your stress. Please remember, you are now living in the **now** '**moment**'.

Accumulated Negative Stress is stress you have experienced over a long period of time. Such stress can accumulate over many years or from your childhood. Accumulated stress is a stress that may need a lot of work to dislodge and move out of your head. By trying the exercise on the previous page, it may help you to start to release such a severe stressor.

Post-traumatic Stress Disorder (PTSD). PTSD can occur after experiencing or witnessing a major trauma. Many military personnel experience this type of stress after being or during the time of military service. Other people may experience this type of stress after:

- Road accidents
- Assault
- Death of a loved one by traumatic circumstances

- Unresolved missing person situation and other traumatic life situations.

Symptoms can include:

- hallucinations, flashbacks, nightmares
- reliving the incident
- avoiding people, places and memories that include part of the trauma
- anger, fits of rage and increased thoughts of hatred
- difficulty in sleeping and guilt feelings.

If you identify with any of the bullet points above, please seek professional help.

If they are suffering any form of PTSD, young children may experience bed wetting, and delays in the development of motor skills.

Acute Stress within acute stress, a person may experience the feeling of a lack of reality, life is just an existence. A person may feel they are not really living in the world as it is. They may experience 'brain fog'. Brain fog is a cognitive deficit, which includes:

- Difficulty in processing incoming information from either reading or heard information
- Forgetfulness, memory recall, and confusion
- Difficulty in long and short-term planning
- Learning difficulties
- Disorganisation in your work or home space
- Difficulty in paying attention to incoming information

- You feel sluggish, you are not 'with it!
- You may experience, difficulty in finding the words to say or have a lack of understanding in what people are saying.

When I was conducting the research for my book: Devils In Our Food, many food additives (synthetic and otherwise), can and do contribute to 'brain fog'. This was especially noted in eating 'fast food,' 'junk food' and foods high in saturated fat, salt, and sugar.

Junk food containing food additives, appears to contribute to 'Brain Fog' if eaten by students who sit for the end-of-year examinations within Higher Education seem to contribute to a lack of performance within examination outcomes. Over three years, as a senior teacher, teaching psychology, I made observations of my students before and post examination. The questions asked post examination:

- How did you cope?
- What food did you eat prior to the examination?
- Do you think you were prepared?

The relevant question: '*What food did you eat prior to the examination?*' was the key area of interest. Many students had a salad or egg-based meal, while others had gone to a café and eaten hot chips, burgers, fizzy drinks, and junk food meals.

One male student in an examination gave up early and walked out of the room. Prior to the examination, I had seen him in the refectory eating a junk-based meal. He had worked hard for the main part of his studies, was a good student; and to see this happen, as an educator, was heart breaking.

Hypertension is high blood pressure. Hypertension includes:

- Severe headaches
- Shortness of breath
- Feeling the pulsation of your blood flow, and pain in the back of the neck and head
- Severe anxiety

Having been a sufferer of hypertension, in my own experience, it requires urgent professional medical attention. Despite all I have written about stress, this one heading sends me directly to the doctor for instant medical help and support.

Things to avoid when experiencing hypertension:

- Excessive salt
- Alcohol
- Smoking
- Drug taking and
- Extra stress.

Like so many people, I too, need to manage stress. Age has its benefits. I now know not drink much alcohol, maybe half a glass on a Friday and Saturday night, I do not smoke and do not take drugs, but at times in my life, I need to manage hypertension.

The key to managing stress is looking and caring for yourself.

Key areas:

- Eat a healthy diet.
- Understand, all stress areas and that stress is a health condition and a condition that needs to be taken seriously. By taking care of yourself, it is done through love and understanding of yourself.
- Be open to yourself and admit that you are experiencing stress. Being 'macho' and denying stress is not healthy or wise.
- Give yourself quality rest.
- Spend quality time with your friends and family.
- Learn about stress and stress management.
- Develop hobbies and interests other than those that are work related.
- Exercise regularly.
- Be responsible for your condition, share your experiences with friends and family but do not bore them with the topic.
- Avoid eating 'junk food' this will only add to your stress and will destroy all the good work you are doing.
- Avoid smoking, alcohol, and drug abuse and lastly,
- Learn to love yourself, and who you are unconditionally.

If you are not happy with who you are and what you are carrying around in your head because of past experiences, learn to release the pain and work with the Key areas of stress outlined in the above.

As part of managing stress, I will take you breathing techniques further in the book.

More about the interaction of the ego personality states

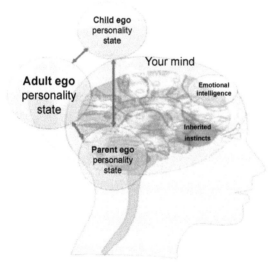

The Parent ego personality state may interact with the Adult ego personality state and reprimand you if you do something illogical or foolish. For instance, spending money on a credit card and you cannot pay the bill when it arrives!

The Adult ego personality state stays in control, but it could weaken if the Child ego personality state has its way and you buy what you cannot afford!

The Child ego personality state will want you to spend regardless of how tight or short money is!

With an understanding of how you can interact with your ego personality states you can avoid many difficult and, in some instances, embarrassing situations such as spending money when you cannot afford to. By taking definite action, you keep your mind and body free of stress.

Working with your ego personality states at acceptable times

Using acceptable Child or Parent ego personality states does not become intimidating or embarrassing, if for example: when a person is experiencing the death of a loved one, grief, accident, or illness. In these instances, people need to work with empathy and understanding of what another person is experiencing. For instance, you may get a glass of water for a person who feels sick during your club meeting, this is working from your Parent and Adult ego personality states. Or you are walking down the road where some children are playing with a ball. The ball comes your way, and you take the opportunity to kick or catch it. The children, for a short time only, have a bit of fun returning the ball to you, you are now working with the Child ego personality state.

The setting and situation of the communication and interaction are important ingredients within the *mix* of the communication and the emotion taking place at the time.

At different times in life, and as adults, we need to work with the situation and experiences of the time.

Showing empathy and respect for our family, neighbours, community, and the world community comes about by working with and understanding how we each, use the information and working components inside our heads. By taking this positive action, we work for the benefit of all humankind.

Muck-Up days – final year for high school students

However, despite age, young people can and do get into trouble. End of Year, Muck-Up days. Recently emerging in our high schools and in the media headlines: Muck-Up days. Muck-up days have been a part of a tradition for many schools in Australia. This year, however, has shown a divisive and sinister attempt to humiliate members of the public. Earlier on in the book, I have spoken of maturation. Clearly, these high school students are not mature. Muck-Up[19] days include a number of stunts, that are both diabolical, dangerous and break the law. Muck-Up days have a list of scavenger hunts, these hunts include humiliating activities for the student and unsuspecting members of the public.

---

[19] /www.smh.com.au/national/nsw

When the young adult shows childish tendencies

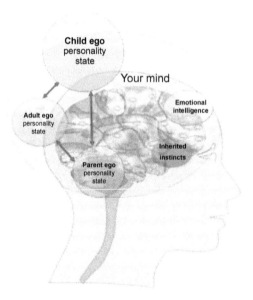

The initiating students of the scavenger hunts to take place would, like many criminal activities, work from the Child ego personality state. Mentioned in the Sydney Morning Herald article was a student's apology, after the act was done. During committing the act, he worked with his Child ego personality state. With the apology, he worked with his Adult ego personality state. Within the apology, the question needs to be asked, 'is he sincere or is his Child ego personality state playing with his mind...?' – has he learnt his lesson, or will he commit a stupid act again in the future?

If the student goes on to commit stupid acts again and again, maturity has not taken place. The Child ego personality state will want more fun in the future, if this happens, can then become a sinister mind game.

When there is a lack of maturity interacting within an individual's ego personality states, many games can be played without the person realising they are playing, sometimes, dangerous, and destructive games!

Becoming an Adult

Because a child reaches puberty, grows taller and develops into, what we assume to be an adult body, it cannot be supposed that all adults have indeed reached a stage of mental maturity.

Mental maturity is defined as maturation within most educational institutions or within psychology. Each person's maturation happens at different ages and at different times of their development – some people mentally mature faster than others!

Child ego personality state – maturation levels

A person's maturation level may have many layers within each personality state. Depending on the complexity of the personality, some people may work from deeper and more complicated layers within their ego personality states. Such layers may accumulate from life experiences, culture, customs, and their environment.

If a child does not work through his or her, particular-maturation levels, at their accepted chronological age, they may experience low maturation levels in their adult development. It is difficult to test personal maturation levels in adult human beings because the adult human may have developed other parts of their personality which may allow them to become *cunning* and *street wise.*

If, into the *mix*, we add emotional intelligence, it would suggest that the human mind is indeed a complicated mechanism to understand.

Getting inside your head

We all have times that are favourite times of the week, month, or year. Within the week, it may include your favourite television program or your favourite sports night, it may also include your birthday, thanks-giving day, Christmas, anniversary and so on. At length, I have spoken about the ego personality states of Parent, Adult and Child. Now, let us take this a little deeper.

Within each personality state, there are many layers. I cannot identify the layers you have within each of your personality states, only you can do that. Once you have identified the ego personality state you are working with, you can use this guide to identify how deeply you go within the layers of that state. Let us use the Child ego personality state to identify the layers.

Child ego personality state – its emotional layers

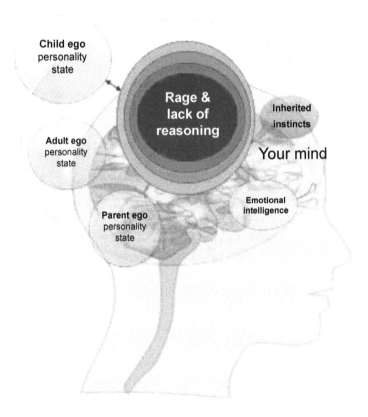

The layers of each person's ego personality state will vary depending on life experiences, culture, personal perception and so on. If you imagine, inside your head you have 'trigger points', something someone does really makes you mad, just so mad…!

It may be the way you, or a member of the family, loads the dishwasher; this seems to be a trigger point in many households!

Or the way he/she washes the car and so the feeling of frustration push into the layers of one of your ego states. If a person goes out of control in the Child ego personality state, it may be characterised as seen in the image on the previous page. You can see, the image of the layers from light pink to dark red. When rage takes over logic can be lost within a person's reasoning.

Identifying the different levels of anger

1. Pink outer circle – it is a niggle, but you can live with it.
2. Deeper pink, second circle, something somebody has done or continues to do, makes you a little angry.
3. Bright red third circle, something happens, or somebody does something and you cannot help yourself, you have to say or do something.
4. Dark red inner circle, you lose it. You explode and lose reasoning you become annoyed or extremely angry.

Within the Adult ego personality state, rage is not seen. The Parent and Child ego personality states may, at times, work together, if this is so, it can become a vile concoction of human evil while in a rage condition.

Hidden rage, revenge and anger can be part of a person's personality, this often shows itself in serial killers, rapists and other criminals and their activities.

At different times, the dominating Parent of Child ego personality states, will or may help to suppress the Adult ego personality state.

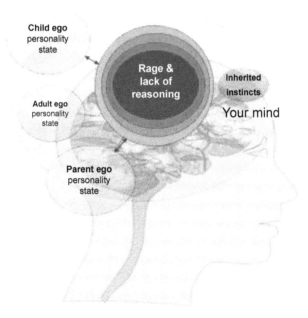

People may live for years keeping hidden anger and the associated reactions under control, but a trigger point may be breached or reached, and the person's personality changes completely.

The image on this page shows how the Child and Parent ego personality states form a pact when they are in the *'I'll get even or revenge'* mode of thinking and action. You can see the Adult ego personality state is not connected to the Child or Parent ego personality states. There is a disconnect from the Adult ego personality state while in such a state of thinking and action!

The model shown on the previous page can be applied to many human behaviours seen in war, criminal gangs with peer intimidation, human acts and atrocities and many more human evil actions.

And so back to the young students Muck-Up days – final year for high school students, if young people were taught about the responsibility they have to themselves, their families, community and where respect is required as part of their social responsibility, we would not see appalling activities within our communities.

Such activities show a lack of mental preparedness for adulthood, this may be caused by a lack of maturation of the biology and physiology of the individual.

A way forward

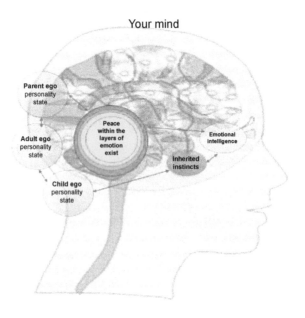

When people experience an understanding of how their mind works within their thinking and how their actions relate to the way their mind works, there is an understanding taking place.

In the last model: A way forward, the layers of emotion are coloured in different tones of green, the ego personality states of Parent Adult and Child are each of a similar size suggesting that the person is suffering less stress and they are in control of their life.

Not all people do Yoga as a stress release exercise, but such a model may be compared when other stress-release activities are undertaken, such as walking, swimming, cycling and or friendly sport is played.

Thought for the day!

Record your feelings throughout the day and write down, once only, when you experienced working with your Parent ego personality state; when you worked from your Adult ego personality state and when you worked from your Child ego personality State.

Working from your Parent ego personality state
....
....

Working from your Adult ego personality state
....
....

Working from your Child ego personality state
....
....

Your Notes
....
....
....
....
....
....

Remember A Time When You
Became Uncontrollably Angry

1) Write down the reason why?
2) Then look at the circles below and try to measure the depth of the anger you experienced.

3) How do you feel about the recollection you have of the experience?

4) Measure your feelings of the experience from 1 – 10

Good……………...Bad
1 2 3 4 5 6 7 8 9 10

Any number between 4, &, 6 identifies you are coping with the memory. Below 4, you have moved on and you are getting on with your life – you no longer have nagging thoughts about the experience.

Above and through 7, 8, 9, and 10, you are beating yourself up over past events – let it go and get on with your life – you can only learn from past experiences!

Remember A Time When
You Felt Peace Within Your Mind and Body

1) Write down the reason when?
2) Then look at the circles below and try to measure the depth of the peace you experienced.

3) How do you feel about the recollection you have of the experience?

4) Measure your feelings of the experience from 1 – 10

Good...............Bad
1 2 3 4 5 6 7 8 9 10

Any number between 4, & 6 identifies you are coping with the memory. Below 4, you are forward and in a positive direction with your thinking and actions.

Above and through 7, 8, 9, and 10, you need to take action to improve your stress levels and learn through growth, and personal development.

When you experience anger that appears to come from nowhere – you just *'blow your stack'* there is a reason for this happening.

You may not be aware of the reason to begin with, but it is there, locked inside your memory and emotions.

If you feel you have hidden anger, please re-read:

Remember A Time When You
Became Uncontrollably Angry

Every time you face your anger, you will start to cope with managing your stress levels.

....

....

....

....

....

....

....

....

....

....

Your Notes

....
....
....
....
....
....
....
....
....
....
....
....
....
....
....
....
....
....
....
....

Unmanaged
stress is a
time bomb
waiting to
explode!

Chapter Six

The Power of Your Mind and The Changes You Make

By putting your mind into a positive gear, you create positive energy, action-filled outcomes.

To make the positive changes in your life, you need to think with positive thoughts.

The essence of positive change can happen once you accept that the power is within your mind and your power is waiting to work with and for you. When stress dominates your life, it can destroy the positive thoughts you have or had and can lead to more negative stress.

A positive mind-set reduces negative stress. Negative stress interferes with the positive mind work you are doing, it also interferes with your mind and body, and is making you sick.

Just one positive thought allows for positive-growth and perception to take place in your life. One positive thought allows for positive changes to take place. Even when a person is facing insurmountable hurdles, positive thinking allows positive changes.

Equally, you have the power to nurture negative stress and allow it to penetrate your life, if this is so, you are allowing that stress to dominate your life. When doing this, you create your own pathway of negativity. Life is too valuable and precious to waste on such a pastime.

Preparing for change

If you have allowed stress to overtake your life, you have created this situation. I know that managing stress for some people will be difficult to do. Some people are susceptible to stress and find managing the condition difficult.

Lisa

Lisa was in her mid-thirties and in a relationship with Ian.

Lisa was new in her marketing job and was facing the challenge of a large marketing campaign for a corporation. Lisa's relationship was not going well, she also had issues with her mother and new manager at work. Her mother thought Ian was a 'good catch' and as her mother had often said, *'... you are in your mid-thirties...'* implying she was getting older if she wanted to have her man and to start her family!

Lisa felt she was not ready to take on such a commitment as marriage! Between Ian, her mother, and the work manager this all added to the stress she was experiencing.

She knew and felt, after not sleeping properly for months, that she was at *'breaking point'*. The feeling of being out of control of her life was adding to the overwhelming feelings she had, which eventually resulted in the first panic attack.

She went to her doctor who wanted to prescribe a mild medication to help to keep her calm, this, she refused to accept.

A few months went by and Lisa had another panic attack, she was convinced she was having a heart attack. She had a thorough medical examination and her physical body was working as it should be.

Finally, she went to a psychologist and heart vascular specialist, both people identified her panic attacks as extreme stress. She was experiencing rapid and light breathing, (hyperventilation), dizziness, anxiety, headaches, and other medical reactions to the stress. She also had the constant feeling of doom.

The doctors identified that Lisa was also prone to stress. For Lisa to have a healthy future, she needs to be brave and take a hard look at her lifestyle.

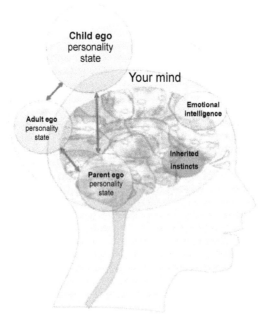

With Lisa's story, she is indecisive and lacks assertiveness. She may be mentally in the same place as a person who is in a state of *'role confusion'*, she needs to be pro-active, but not a bully, to make positive changes. To be decisive, she needs to come from her Adult ego personality state.

Many people live with traditional thinking, like Lisa's mother's implications, *'you need to start your family, or it might be too late…!'* Or she might not really be in love with Ian but has not stated that to him…! Work deadlines in new workplaces can also cause stress to accumulate.

Out of date thinking or traditional thinking?

Because people may live with family rules or folklore that says: *'This is how it's always been.' 'That's the way my family think.' 'My husband wouldn't approve, No, I couldn't do that!' 'I would love to go back to school, but my family believe that a mum's place is in the home!'* Some people find accepting change difficult.

Little do people realise that when demands to stay the same, not to grow or change can and do put demands on another human being. Such demands can cause stress and severe stress problems.

Each person has a responsibility to find their own unique pathway in life. Some people may be denied this natural progression into maturity.

If you want change to happen, you need to accept that you are worthy of fulfilling your destiny and making changes in your life. To change is a birth right; if it is change you want. Change can and does happen, but it might need to be done with compassion. It will, however, take energy, growth, time, and patience – this is staying power!

Where are we now – building the picture?

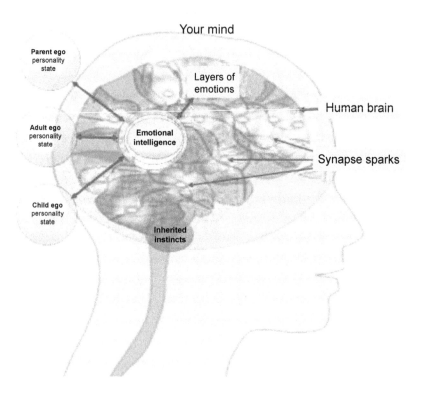

Since and during evolution of the human species, we have been adapting and growing the human brain. Brain growth happens through synapse sparks relaying information from one part of the brain to other parts of the brain. The received information is transferred to other parts of the brain and body for action to be taken.

So far discussed:

1. The human brain
2. The human mind
3. Healthy synapse sparks
4. Berne's ego personality states: Parent, Adult and Child
5. Inherited instincts
6. Emotional intelligence
7. The intensity of emotion.

Please refer to the opposite page.

As I have previously said, we are hard-wired to survive. I do not like to repeat a case study, but I am doing so with the study of Dr Frankl and the Aboriginal people of Australia, both are worth the repetition.

Viktor Frankl's story

Viktor Frankl M.D., PhD. (Born March 26th 1905 Died: Vienna 1997).[20]

Viktor Frankl was a neurologist, psychiatrist, and a Holocaust survivor. Frankl is the founder of Logotherapy.[21] It was due to his

---

[20] Frankl, V 'Man's Search for Meaning' An Introduction to Logotherapy

[21] The theory is founded on the belief that human nature is motivated by the search for a life purpose.

and others' suffering in the concentration camps of World War II that he concluded:

'... that even in the most absurd, painful and dehumanized situation, life has potential and meaning and, therefore that even suffering is meaningful.' He continues: *'... we stumbled on in the darkness, over big stones and through large puddles, along the one road leading from the camp. The accompanying guards kept shouting at us and driving us with the butts of their rifles. Anyone with very sore feet supported himself on his neighbour's arm ...'* One of his neighbours remarked while on the walk: *'... hiding his mouth behind his upturned collar, "if our wives could see us now! I do hope they are better off in their camps and don't know what is happening to us."'*

Logotherapy is an active therapy including the striving to find meaning of your own individual life. Frankl believed that striving to find your meaning to life is the most powerful, motivating and driving force within you.

Frankl's wife was murdered while in one of the concentration camps. He continues: *'I looked at the sky, where the stars were fading, and the pink light of the morning was beginning to spread behind a dark bank of clouds. But my mind clung to my wife's image, imagining it with an uncanny acuteness. I heard her answering me, saw her smile, her frank and encouraging look. Real or not, her look was then more luminous than the sun which was beginning to rise.*

A thought transfixed me: for the first time in my life I saw the truth as it is set into song by so many poets, proclaimed as the final wisdom by so many thinkers. The truth – that love is the ultimate and the highest goal to which man can aspire. Then I grasped the meaning of the greatest secret that human poetry and human thought and belief have to impart: The salvation of man is through love and in love.'

Within Viktor Frankl's immortal words, he continues:

'If a prisoner felt that he could no longer endure the realities of camp life, he found a way out in his mental life – an invaluable opportunity to dwell in the spiritual domain, the one that the SS were unable to destroy. Spiritual life strengthened the prisoner, helped him adapt, and thereby improved his chances of survival.'

With his ultimate vision firmly in his mind, Frankl had the determination to survive the Nazi concentration camp experience. Frankl used his Adult ego personality state and his mature emotional intelligence which allowed him to survive the horrendous ordeals of the Nazi regime.

The human mind can be equally friend or foe; Viktor Frankl made the most of the power of his friend – his mind.

There are many stories of survival where a person has had the internal and mental strength to make the best out of a difficult and destructive situation.

There have been throughout history many determined people that have intuitively worked with their Adult ego personality states.

Just within Australia, in the last bushfires, we saw the brave fire fighters and within our recent history, the brave medical teams who form the 'frontline' workers working with the sick Covid patients and the number of the these workers, who indeed, caught the virus and died doing their duty to the world community.

The human mind is indeed a powerful tool.

The power of the human mind should not be underestimated

In some Australian Aboriginal communities, a personal contract includes living by the mental and cultural conditions of the tribe and is binding. If a member of the tribe commits a severe offence, and a judgment is given by the elders – it could mean certain death for the perpetrator.

The perpetrator is not hanged or beheaded: nobody takes their life through suicide or other destructive acts.

Within the Aboriginal culture, the perpetrator would kill him or herself with the power of his or her own mind. A simple act of *Pointing the Bone* in the direction of the condemned meant he or she would go into the bush and slowly, little by little, stage by stage, slow their bodily functions down.

Through their cultural values, the individual accepts the mental conditions within their tradition. Their acceptance of the tradition gives them the ability to slowly stop their lungs, heart, and other vital bodily functions from working, and then they die.

In some form or other, each of the two above studies have a contractual aspect attached. Viktor Frankl was determined that the Nazi regime would not own or take over his mind and then outlined was the moral code of the Aboriginal people of Australia.

Personal contracts – human contracts

These two last studies alone identify the power we each hold within our heads. Each person has the power to commit atrocities, survive unbelievable human pain and ordeals and the power to slowly, if told, to end their life, regardless of age or culture!

Every human contract lived out is owned by the owner. In this instance, you make a contract with yourself to finish reading this book because you want to know more – this is a simple contract, but nonetheless, it is a contract.

Once there is an understanding of the power of the human mind, people will respect this very good mental tool that can be used to benefit humankind and not the destruction of innocent individuals or groups of people who live by different values or belief systems.

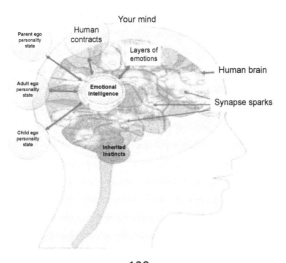

Each of the ego personality states can carry contracts. In the study of Victor Frankl, he has worked with his Adult ego personality state – he was determined to survive his ordeal.

From a culture of over forty-thousand years, the Aboriginal people of Australia live within their life code, history, and belief systems and have identified the power of the human mind.

Mental contracts, held within the human mind, are not only used by human beings to commit atrocities; they are also used to create good and positive outcomes. It is the new dawning with research on human behaviour. As you read on, and from the thinking you do, you are now aware, that the number of good people in the world outweigh the number of cruel people!

Within any human contract, whether for good or evil purposes, there are different levels of *stress* operating within the individual.

Thought for the day!

Think of one positive idea: how could you use a mental contract to help you to create one good outcome in your life? Just one good thought will reduce your *stress* levels.

Write it down.

....

....

....

....

Good human mental contracts are used by people when they want to build their home, write a book, lose weight, go on a pilgrimage, find a cure for cancer, and other benefits for themselves, the family, the greater human race, the planet, its flora and fauna.

You use mental contracts every day of your life: you have a mental contract to go to work to earn money, you make a light mental contract to cut the grass today, every positive step taken with commitment is a contract.

For example, you make a contract with your employer, your business, your farm, and other forms of paid work – paid work allows you to financially survive and bring the money home which helps to keep going and have a good life. Each, and every person works to some form of contract, personal or otherwise!

If a person has a calling to work as a missionary, aid worker or as in the case of *Mother Teresa,* in her commitment to help the sick, poor, orphaned and the dying throughout India and went on to do more missionary work in other countries.

Each, and every calling, regardless of the type of work, is a form of personal contract.

Olympians and sports people make personal contract when they enter the sports arena to win a race, throw the javelin the furthest and so on. I write contracts for myself when I want or need to write a book.

It is the level of the contract you are aspiring to and from which position you come from when making the contract that makes the difference. You will need to ask yourself: '... *am I coming from the Parent, Adult or Child ego personality state when making this contract?'*

For, the purpose, of showing you the power of mental contracts, think about something small but positive that you would like to commit to and see through to its completion.

Thought for the day

From the understanding you have gained by reading this chapter, you will be aware that you are in control of how you use your Mind. You can use your Mind to create both negative and positive outcomes for yourself. Working with a Personal Contract for positive outcomes will reduce your stress levels and support you in many different life situations.

Your Notes

....

....

....

....

....

If you do not intend to keep the Contract on the following page, please do not sign it.

The Contract

We underestimate the power of mental contracts. We have become accustomed to signing contracts that are written on paper and usually produced by the legal profession.

This is a foolish error!

Mental contracts are powerful tools – we have seen this power in the recent terrorist attacks in Martin Place, Sydney, Australia and Paris, France. We have all seen the atrocities of the wars in Africa and the individual grotesque acts by terrorists on the innocent. These barbaric acts would not have taken place if the perpetrator/s had not made a mental contract.

Equally so, contracts can be used for great good and accomplishment – athletes win at the Olympics because they have a commitment and a human contract in place!

(In the following chapters I will introduce to a new and exciting area of your mind within the Orders of Self, Family and Work.)

Your Notes

....
....
....
....
....
....
....
....
....
....
....
....
....
....
....
....
....
....
....
....
....

Unmanaged stress is a time bomb waiting to explode!

Chapter Seven

Emotional Intelligence, Personal Contracts, Self, Family and Work –

The beginning of understanding emotional intelligence and the Orders within Self, Family and Work

I have outlined in Chapter Six the power of mental contracts. As described, the contract can be used for both good (positive) and evil (negative) outcomes.

If you allow your mind to go on aimlessly without any direction and guidance, then you may be heading for trouble or into difficult times, you will also add to your stress levels.

When your mind takes on the role of the foe – the enemy, it only does so because you have given it the permission to do so. When you read this for the first time and realise this is possibly what has happened in a previous event or events in your life, you may experience or feel overcome by such a realisation; it may also come as a surprise!

There is always a lot going on inside your head!

We are not taught at school about our brain or our mind; this lack of preparation can lead many people into difficult times as they grow and mature into adulthood.

A progression of thinking

Negative thoughts have ways of encroaching on your good mind and raising your stress levels. (extracted from my original book: (*Adam's Mind – Eve's Psyche'*).

To begin:

1) You will have one negative thought – it is fleeting and comes and goes within a nano-second.
2) You may retrieve that thought – this then becomes the seed of the thought!
3) You may now give that thought, the seed, two seconds of your time and then dismiss it again.
4) Something happens to upset you and you feel frustrated and annoyed.
5) You may then go to the pub, club, or sit and *stew things over*. You also drink alcohol or take drugs to relieve how you feel – this is a mistake!
6) The negative thought, now a seed, is on its way to germination and growth.
7) The negative seed occupies more of your time.
8) The seed is becoming entrenched in your thinking, and that is all you start to think about.
9) The seed and thoughts you have – have life – you have given birth to this negativity and it is in your head – it becomes a real and living part of you.
10) The negative seed and the attached thoughts start to live with you – you may become obsessive with the way you are thinking. You may develop Obsessive Compulsive Thinking (OCT) and Obsessive, Compulsive Disorder (OCD) –

obsessive behaviour may be the outcome because of one negative thought!

Each, and every person has a capacity to develop negative thoughts that lead to negative ideas and destructive outcomes – terrorism is but one outcome!

You can make your mind the enemy and by doing so, you become the slave, the prisoner of your own mind. This thinking may contribute to a mental health condition.

Once you accept this form of negative thinking you may lock yourself into a mental prison sentence – the prison is without bars. The sentence stifles your life energy, and you learn to live a miserable life and accept a miserable life as *your lot* in life! That is not how it should be.

Being your own prisoner, with exception of biological mental illness, is simple to achieve, you just keep feeding into your mind negative messages such as:

- *'I'm no good*
- *I can't do anything*
- *I'm hopeless*
- *That is too good for me*
- *I don't deserve to be healthy*
- *I don't deserve to be wealthy*
- *I don't deserve a better job*
- *I don't deserve to have the right partner in my life*
- *I deserve to have this pain*
- *I'm not worthy! It is all his/her fault.*

- *I need a cause to understand my worthiness (as in the mind of the terrorist)*
- *By creating this negativity and fear, I have power over other people*

This last bullet point can be seen in bullies in the workplace, some employers, terrorists, drug criminals and criminals.

Each negative thought you have can lead to a destructive outcome if you are not in control of your thinking. Negative thinking adds to your negative stress levels and leads to raised blood pressure, headaches, and a shorter life span.

Other negative thoughts may include:

- *That is not good enough it needs to be done to perfection!*

On a positive note, in some instances, perfection is the ultimate of attainment, but generally, and in life, your best ability is all that is required or needed! It is the learning processes you go through while trying to do your best that eventually creates a perfect outcome.

If you persist in allowing negative thoughts to germinate to seeds, the negative messages will build up in your mind putting layer upon layer, depth upon depth of rubbish down that becomes ever more difficult to remove. Negative thoughts may germinate quickly if you are carrying elements of anger in your thinking.

The mental rubbish you are collecting overtakes your thinking and your personality changes; you are no longer the person you were intended to be at your birth and when you started out on your journey through life.

People learn to live with these negative conditions, some not realising they can change and go from a negative life state to positive life outcomes just by changing the way they think!

The way you think forms your attitude.

Taking the initiative

There are many displaced people in the world – they are refugees looking to call a place home. Some of these refugees risk their lives to start again. They travel in overcrowded boats, behind compartments or containers of dangerous liquids and materials on trucks or lorries – they lie close to the wheels, in concealed cavities of aircraft, just to gain freedom and a livelihood.

These people have seen murder, pain, their homes, and families blown apart; they have possibly seen more bloodshed and destruction than many of us will ever experience in a lifetime.

Eve

After a busy day of work, we often hear about atrocities when we catch up with the 6.00 or 7.00pm news on television. Or we might see something written in social or print media.

On a warm sunny, summers afternoon, the story of Eve unravelled in a classroom in the South of England.

While teaching I met Eve. Eve grew up in Eastern Europe.

After a class one day, both Eve and I took some time out to have a chat, this was a spontaneous reaction by both of us. Eve wanted to talk.

Eve lived through and witnessed the uprising in Kosovo. Eve witnessed horrific atrocities, she saw her parents murdered, and saw her town burnt to the ground.

Eve had been a student at the time of the uprising and experienced severe stress and trauma. She managed to escape and made her way to Britain. When she returns to her native town, she says, *'... many of my friends still live in the newly built town and continually talk about the atrocities that took place.'*

At the time of us talking, Eve was completing her university studies. Since living in England, she has married and has a family. She works as a teacher, and continues, *'... it's happened, you cannot change what has happened, but you need to get on with life ...'*

Eve's a brave woman and has the determination not to let the past dictate the present or her future, or the future of her family.

Eve works from her Adult ego personality state and into the *mix* she uses her emotional intelligence, while staying in control of her memories and the pain she feels.

During our conversation, I could see the pain in her face and eyes. She experiences nostalgia and grief times, but she knows these times are part of the healing she needs to go through. The grief process helps her to cleanse any negative feelings that, if allowed to permeate, could become destructive to her wellbeing, and interfere with the life she has built for herself, her family and her future in Britain.

Eve has been back to her town, which has been re-built, and some of her friends still live in the town, including her best friend. Her best friend has not moved on.

People can become 'mentally stuck'. Becoming 'mentally stuck' does not allow a person to grow out of a traumatic situation. To help people survive a trauma; positive mental growth needs to take place.

If a person is not ready to change, another person cannot persuade them to change, change needs to happen from within the individual.

Eve continually works with her Adult ego personality state and with her positive emotional intelligence

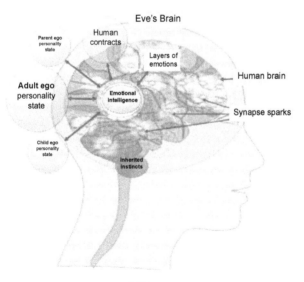

While Eve works with her Adult ego personality state and her emotional intelligence, she manages her emotions and the past pain she has experienced. It would also appear that Eve has positive human contracts in place. This management allows her to effectively carry on her new life.

Eve's best friend

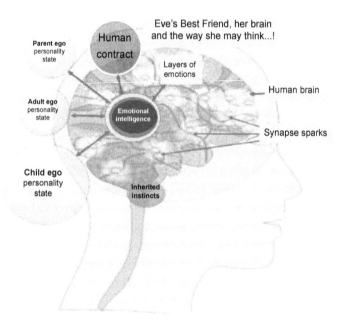

It is not within the realm of this book to pass judgement on any one person, but through pictures that relate to, particular-life experiences, we can see that different people experience different traumas in different ways.

In the above model, Eve's best friend's Child personality ego state may be playing a large role in the way she is managing her grief and loss. She may also be committed to a human contract that does not allow her to grow, therefore, her emotional intelligence is kept stifled.

Effective communication cannot take place while Eve's friend is 'mentally stuck' in the Child Ego Personality State.

You can see by the description on the previous pages and the study of Eve, how many people can and do become 'mentally stuck' with destructive and hurtful past experiences.

Eve values her friend and realises the situation. Eve now communicates with her friend's Child ego personality state, this is the only way the friendship can continue to survive at this time.

This is a harsh realisation, Eve's friend may one day realise that the past is the past, but she alone, will have to accept it and take the responsibility for owning her **Now** and current time and her future.

Through Eve making the choice to mentally move with her ego personality states, her friendship is intact, and she maintains her connections to her homeland.

Eve has made it her intention: *'… to move on with her life…'*

Understanding how we can manage the way we individually think will allow for a greater awareness of human action, reaction, and behaviour and the stress attached to each emotion.

It is the start of understanding – Eve and her friend

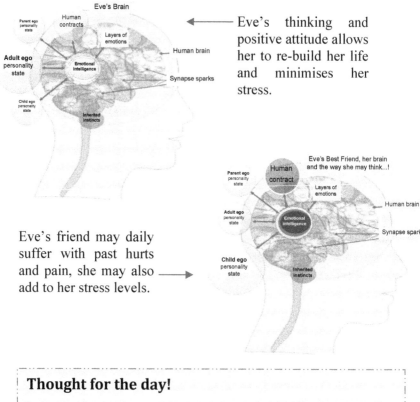

Eve's thinking and positive attitude allows her to re-build her life and minimises her stress.

Eve's friend may daily suffer with past hurts and pain, she may also add to her stress levels.

Thought for the day!

Think of a benefit you could gain by working from your Adult ego personality state – write it down

....

....

....

Emotional intelligence

You will recall reading in Chapter Five how Charles Darwin in the 1800s had identified *emotional expression*; Thorndike's research on *social intelligence* in the 1920s, Howard Gardner's work describing *multiple intelligence* in 1983 and Daniel Golman's book in 2000, introducing *traits and ability.* Through my research and writing I now expand on Eric Berne's Model of the three Ego Personality States.

I have further identified *that emotional intelligence is a combination of* **Self**, **Family** and **Work** within your ego personality states. Further research identifies how you can mix and match different personality characteristics into the way you think and behave. These characteristics include:

The Orders within Self, Family and Work.

Self, Family and Work

The Orders or layers within our personalities relate to:

- Our personality traits
- Our life experiences
- Habits
- Attitudes
- Culture and
- Upbringing.

Through this identification we have the ability, to work with our mind to create the life and future we want.

Emotional intelligence and their three symbolic, figurative shapes

To keep the understanding of emotional intelligence and the ego personality states identified, emotional intelligence can be seen through three symbolic shapes. Each shape plays a unique role in your life.

Each shape identifies: You, Your Family, and the Work you do.

Each of the shapes works with different emotional levels within your emotional intelligence.

Emotional intelligence within Self, Family and Work

Each of the above symbols are uniquely different because each shape symbolises a different part of your life and personality. These features are you. You are a combination of the above: **Self, Family** and **Work**.

Most people are fortunate to have a Family in their life – if you do not have a direct family you may include neighbours and friends as family.

I recently went back to England for a nine-day catch-up with the family and loved ones. On the trip, I was determined to catch up with my elderly Aunty. She was the last remaining person in that generation of that time. As we sat talking, she told me about the charity work she was doing at the church. She had always said, 'I'm retired.' When I pointed out, '…but you are still working…!' my aunt looked in astonishment. Because her work was unpaid, she did not see it as work.

Even if you are retired, you will still have areas in your life which are classed as work. Sadly, this beautiful lady died, earlier this year, 2020.

Starting with Self

Self

The Self needs to contain:

- Confidence
- Positive self-esteem
- Personal values
- Culture
- Morality (a morality base)
- Personal traits (personal characteristics)
- Self-sustainability and

- Personal growth (as you read through the book, you may wish to add more to this list).

Within all cultures, different human history, and backgrounds, the three areas of existence within Self, Family and Work are of the utmost importance.

Within this explanation, the shape of the triangle of Self is no accident. The triangle represents you as Self and the role you play in the Family and the Work you do. Self, Family and Work are the very fabric of most people and the human society of the world we live in.

Starting with Self and by taking each shape within your emotional intelligence separately, you will gain a greater understanding of how your emotions and ego personality states work together – these will be spoken of and then expanded on as you read through the book.

Your emotional intelligence may vary daily because of the different life demands you experience. Your experiences incorporate your wellbeing and health, lifestyle, family, career, or work.

Family

A Family base needs to be:

- Secure
- Comforting
- Warm
- Loved
- Cherished
- Friendly
- Happy
- Belonging (with a sense of belonging)
- Protected and
- Home.

Within the existence of the Family there are celebrations for happy events or grief when a close family member becomes sick or dies and other rites of passage[22] that exist for all people.

The '0' or significant birthdays such as 20, 21, 30, 40, 50, 60, 70, 80 or other rites of passage including, weddings, funerals, anniversaries within your close relationships, all impact on your emotional intelligence and your stress levels at the time they happen.

Other contributing factors which alter or influence your emotional intelligence are the foods and drink you consume daily; the stress of the work or job you do, your financial or family concerns and other related worries.

---

[22] A person's personal passage through life. It includes, birth, marriage, divorce, significant coming of age celebrations and finally, death.

Work

In Work you need to have:

- The skills and ability to do the job
- Be confident about the work you are doing
- To have the ability to communicate effectively
- Show you have initiative and
- Be dependable.

Introducing your emotional intelligence – Self, Family, Work, and their Four Orders – First Order

Within each of Self, Family and Work there are Four Orders. These Orders can be powerful friends or destructive enemies!

Self – First Order

To give this shape and Self the First Order is not a selfish act or an act of vanity or narcissism. You are identifying with who you are as a person and that you have your own qualities, values, goals, and aspirations.

The Self is the only person you have any control over. Simply put, you can and should only want to control your own emotions, feelings, actions, and life relationships. It is not acceptable behaviour for another person to assume or perceive ownership of another adult person. This, is why, the Self is the First Order. You own who you are, and are accountable, and responsible for the words you say and the actions you do or take.

The Self is the control base – you are with the Self 24/7, year after year, from inception to death.

The Self is the combination of:

- Your life experiences, both negative and positive
- Cultural background including tradition and ideals
- Habits, both negative and positive
- Behaviours both good and bad
- Ideas and attitudes, also both negative and positive and
- Your emotional base.

The Self needs to be:

- Protected
- Guarded
- Well nourished
- Respected
- Positively looked after and
- Well maintained.

Maintaining your Self to your full capacity takes eating healthily, exercise, understanding how your mind and body works, discipline and determination. By maintaining the Self, you will gain the greatest maximum and positive outcomes from your life.

By maintaining Self, you care for your yourself.

Self – First Order – Family

It is the understanding of your priorities that allows you to understand how to manage stress.

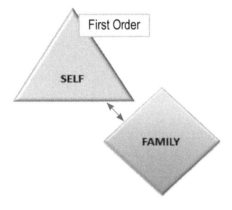

When the Self works in the First Order – Family, there is resilience and dedication.

Families often go through crisis: because of business closures, parents may lose their jobs. Many good and viable businesses suffer during the times of recession, depression and in 2020, the Covid pandemic. Homes may be threatened because of unpaid mortgages, the family debt may become unmanageable. Through all negative experiences, the family suffers, this suffering leads to the family experiencing stress.

Other stressful events happen when our children grow and become teenagers and decide to leave home, this can add to the stress of the parents.

Sometimes and within the Family base, positive foundations may be shaken because of the changes taking place through divorce, illness, separation, sickness, or death.

The once-settled Family unit, can at times, be totally up-ended, uprooted, and disintegrate. What was once, a safe and comfortable place no longer exists for the individuals of the Family! Regardless of what happens, the family is still the family and a family bond can continue.

If the base of the Family is built on love, many difficult times can be managed more effectively; a more destructive element to the Family base is the death of a parent. Again, secure love can help to bridge this difficult time.

Through ordinary times, when you are working with Self – First Order, Family, you maintain the responsibility for your younger dependents, and other family members. You maintain continuity in your life and the lives within the family. You keep secure your love life and the love for your Family base.

When you are working with Self – First Order, Family there is enough leverage to allow younger family members, such as teenage children, the opportunity to expand and grow with their own unique life experiences.

At a later date, a fractured or broken family has a better chance of coming together if there is an established base of:

- Virtue
- Quality
- Family values
- Honesty
- Loyalty and
- Worth.

The above can and is achieved through working with and developing your Self – First Order and Family.

Through difficult and traumatic times, a pre-established base provides a source of bonding, that without, it is difficult to repair broken or damaged Family relationships.

When you are comfortable with Self – First Order and if a relationship comes to its natural end, you will have the confidence to walk away from the situation and know that the relationship was for a *limited time only!*

You have, through the experience, the opportunity to take from the gained knowledge the positive outcomes and the opportunity to leave the relationship where it finished.

In order to grow, and often with family members involved, there are times when the family or family member, break all of the pre-conceived and sometimes ineffective rules of the familiar Family base. The base appears to crumble before your very eyes. This may be an extremely painful and stressful experience for those people who are unfamiliar with the natural cycle that some human beings need to go through in order to follow their own unique road map, destiny or their natural pathway within natural law.

Natural Law

Within natural law the theory poses that all humans possess intrinsic values that govern reasoning and behaviour. The law may be seen, as a structure of the universe as opposed to being developed by human beings. In other words: *natural law may be inherited at birth,* however, through conditioning and the environment a person lives within, the understanding of natural law is either dismissed or not understood.

Self – First Order – Work

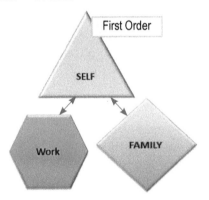

When you are working with Self – First Order – Work, you are able:

- To see reasoning
- Be responsible for your action or actions and outcomes
- See difficulties before they arise
- Make value judgement decisions

- Be accountable
- To have the ability to delegate and give guidance
- See the human potential in others
- Face difficult situations
- Give valued direction to others
- Be focused and dedicated to the work at hand
- Allow others to make valued decisions
- To take-into-account, other people's points of view
- Allow leadership potential to emerge in other people
- To have the ability to let go when it is time to let go.

You have the ability, while at work, to take ownership, of yourself, and the environment within which you work. This does not mean you become a bully by comparison, you have the ability, to manage, and work within certain guidelines and criteria. You are dependable, mature and may see opportunities arise before they arise. You find positive life energy, see the learning needed and the personal growth potential in every situation – you also find the *challenge* of each new day and more.

By the private work you do on Self, you effectively manage your stress levels. You know when to stop, take a rest and then start again.

The model on the opposite page shows how we work with three different parts of our personality within the different areas of our lives.

Thought for the day!

With SELF, FAMILY and WORK in the **First Order** list one action in each of SELF, FAMILY and WORK that could improve your wellbeing and reduce your stress levels.

SELF:..

....

....

FAMILY:...

....

....

WORK:..

....

....

....

....

....

....

....

How can you use a personal contract to make positive changes in your life?

Second Contract
Self, Family and Work – First Order

Write it down how you identify with Self.

....

What can you do to benefit Self?

....

Write down how you identify with Self and Family

....

What can you do to benefit Self and Family?

....

Write down how you identify with Self and Work.

....

What can you do to benefit Self and Work?

....

Date..

Signature..

Using change in your life – you may wish to come back to this later in the book

How can you benefit yourself through working with and using the information in the last chapter?

Please write your thoughts down.

....

....

....

With the understanding you have of Self, Family and Work, how can you make the necessary changes and work with the changes needed as identified in your contract in the previous chapter?

....

....

....

....

....

....

....

....

Your Notes

....
....
....
....
....
....
....
....
....
....
....
....
....
....
....
....
....
....
....
....
....

Unmanaged stress is a time bomb waiting to explode!

Chapter Eight

The Power of Emotional Intelligence, the Orders Within Self, Family and Work, and Your Memory

Following on from the previous Chapters we have discussed:

1) Your mind
2) Your brain
3) Positive synapse sparks that allow information to flow and, if required, action to take place
4) Your inherited instincts
5) Parent ego personality state
6) Adult ego personality state
7) Child ego personality state
8) Your emotional intelligence
9) Layers of emotions
10) Self
11) Family
12) Work
13) Human contracts and now, your
14) Memories

Of course, none of the above would happen or take place if your memory is not working. Memories start working with your inherited instinct from an early age during your mother's pregnancy.

By the time we reach maturity, both physically and mentally, about the age of twenty-five, we have a collection of information that is stored in our memory banks and each memory is either: good (positive) bad (negative) or something that has produced learning. Even negative memories provide a source of learning that may be accessed by you either now or at some time in the future.

Emotional intelligence within our memories – Self, Family and Work

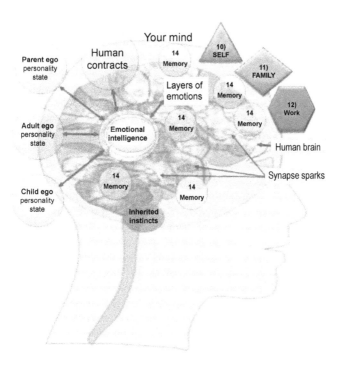

To make the understanding easier of how our mind and brain work together, the symbols above are figurative to give you some idea of how we take in and store information in the memories. Each piece of information received, triggers a reaction by you. The interpretation of collected experiences and memories will vary from person to person. No two people will ever see the same action, word spoken or feel the same emotionally about one single and same event. Each person's perception is different, and each memory relates to either, Self, Family or Work.

You are doing a lot of work to collect the information, (which become your tools), these tools will build up in your mental toolbox. Once learnt, you can retrieve these tools from your memory at any time. By using this information continuously, you learn how to work positively with your mind to keep yourself safe from harm, build more mind tools, and have the ability, to manage stress.

Human memory

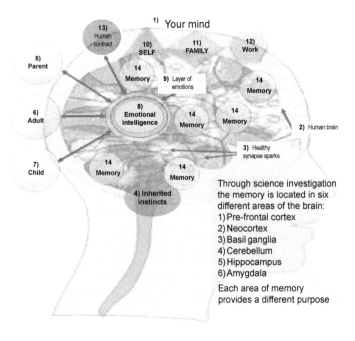

1) Your mind

13) Human contract

10) SELF
11) FAMILY
12) Work

5) Parent

14 Memory
9) Layer of emotions
14 Memory

6) Adult

8) Emotional intelligence
14 Memory
14 Memory

2) Human brain

3) Healthy synapse sparks

7) Child

14 Memory
14 Memory

4) Inherited instincts

Through science investigation the memory is located in six different areas of the brain:
1) Pre-frontal cortex
2) Neocortex
3) Basil ganglia
4) Cerebellum
5) Hippocampus
6) Amygdala

Each area of memory provides a different purpose

165

Through the advancement of technology, we are now able to see so much more within the human body and brain. This technology allows us to see how synapse sparks work when we each experience different stimuli from our environment. Different areas of memory work with different stimulus.

Through science investigation, we now know that human memories, are located, in six different areas of the brain:

1) Pre-frontal cortex
2) Neocortex
3) Basil ganglia
4) Cerebellum
5) Hippocampus
6) Amygdala

Each area of memory provides a different purpose and works for different outcomes to meet your needs.

The human memory works in conjunction with the outlined numbered parts of the brain, as seen on the previous page and above. The figurative shapes shown help us to understand and formulate some ideas of how the human mind and brain work together. Thus, giving us an idea of how we each individually think and work.

Base-memories, which include inherited instincts, are stored, some when in the womb, and may be retrieved later in life. Memories are continually built through childhood, adolescence and continually through adulthood.

While in the womb, the unborn child becomes familiar when hearing their mother's voice. This familiarity may be part of the bonding that takes place at birth.

Human psyche also plays a role in the way we think, act, and perceive incoming information. Your human psyche may include your emotional intelligence and or associated retentions within your DNA.

Most people have had an experience, *'this doesn't feel good'* or, *'...this feels strangely familiar...'* or*'...what he or she is saying, doesn't sit comfortably with me...!'*

When you work with your memory, emotional intelligence, and psyche, you start to work with your intuition. Your intuition contains:

- Moral truth
- Truth
- Intuition comes about by using your mind, in particular intuitive ways.

Both intuition and emotional intelligence need from you:

- Respect
- Understanding
- Being looked after
- Acknowledgement
- Time
- Commitment and the
- Positive mental input of whole, good information.

Because so little is known about how each individual person's emotional intelligence and mind work, no one formula, list of *'how to'* or prescribed steps, will be right for everybody – it just cannot be. We are not clones' we are individual people.

Each person is unique and has a different personality, a different set of characteristics, history, perceptions, national and family culture, and a different set of goals and values. There will be a cross-over and some people will assimilate with one another, but no two people will ever think exactly as the other!

When you have been in the environment of people who don't have the same set of thinking or life values as you, you may feel uncomfortable and may want to or feel the need to leave that environment.

Assimilation

Equally so, if you have assimilated with people and you have adopted another person or group's philosophy, you may find you have received wrong or destructive input information; you may have experienced the negative outcome of that particular process.

Many people assimilate, this is seen in cult followings, and other group meetings who follow an idea, ideal or philosophy.

The inner voice

How often have you denied listening to your inner voice? The inner voice, I believe, combines with our intuition to keep us safe and to fulfil our life's role.

Once again, if you feel you are in a negative life situation, your mind has been receiving negative messages from you, you always feel angry and blame other people for where you are now; you may have blocked out your inner voice. Such an inner voice appears to come when we are still and giving our mind, the respect it deserves.

In my experience, the inner voice may tell me: *'I am in the wrong place at the wrong time!'* Your inner voice is attached to your internal messaging service. Your messaging service may give you new ideas, steps to take to reach your goal and more. As you start to understand how your mind works, you will start to understand how assimilation can sometimes be the wrong move for you.

When you start to work with your emotional intelligence, you will learn to listen to the internal messages you are given or sent. As you learn, you will start to understand why possible assimilation with other people or situations can sometimes get you into trouble!

Your emotional intelligence is your friend; it only works for you and when listened to, works for your wellbeing. Your emotional intelligence works with your sub-conscious mind 24/7 – it is, indeed, an intrinsic part of who you are.

Back to Self – Family – Second Order

There is indeed a lot going on inside our heads. When I am writing a book or if I look back at a book, I might say to my husband or children, *'I don't know how I have written this or that book!'* The way we each work with our mind, still amazes me.

In the previous Chapter I spoke about SELF, FAMILY and WORK and the First Order. It is now time to talk about the Second Order and how it works with your personality states of Parent, Adult and Child.

The Second Order is productive – it gets things done. It is active and looking for the next challenge or job to do.

Self – Second Order

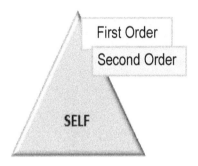

I research and write my books in the Second Order. I also clean the house, cook the meals, write the birthday cards, if needed, in this Order. In this Order, you are not ready to sit down and watch television. It is your leisure time and you may play tennis or golf or make a batch of biscuits, have a shower, wash your hair, make the children's lunches and more – you are into production and work.

The Second Order is when you make decisions and act on that decision. You may drive your car, give the car a wash if dirty and so on. You may decide to buy another home and find yourself driving around the neighbourhood that afternoon looking at the houses for sale.

The Second Order is where you get your mind ready and prepare to take action with the Family.

Self – Second Order – Family

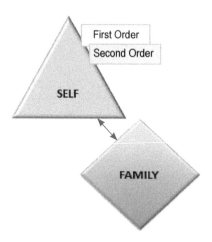

In this Order, the Family is productive, you are working with Self for the positive benefit of the Family. You may decide to go for a camping trip, pack the car with the camping gear and be ready to go!

In this Order, the caring part of Self reaches out to other members of the Family when there is pain or sickness in the Family. The Self works to create beautiful meals and surprise birthday parties for another member of the Family. The Family may include brothers, sister, cousins, neighbours who are close, and who you have bonded with.

The Self – Second Order – Family may have a best friend and if that friend is in financial need, the Self, in this Order may help until the friend is financially back on their feet.

The Self and Family may include extended family members, which happens when divorce takes place or when a person remarries after a partner has died.

Self – Second Order – Work

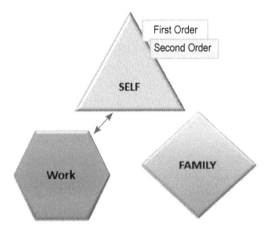

The Self in the Second Order – Work wants to get things done. If you work for yourself and you are working from this Order, you are *action* plus. You may book and attend trade shows, spend hours looking at You Tube to get different ideas of how to build something that you can use in the business. Over the weekend, you have come up with an idea, you spend the weekend building a prototype ready to show your staff on Monday morning. You want to see action and progress.

If you work for a boss, you want to do your job to your best ability, you are willing to share your ideas at the next staff meeting. You may work late into the night to finish a project that you know will help the business expand.

Positive and transitional stress

When you are in the Self – Second Order - Work, you are working with positive and transitional stress. If you are coping with life and become stressed because of family problems, relationship problems, your stress is lowered while in the Second Order and the productive way you are working.

Simply said, while working as you are, your mind is on the work you are doing, and not on other worrying or other concerns in your life.

In Self – Second Order – Work, your emotional intelligence is working effectively with your Adult ego personality. It is the combination of working with your Adult ego personality state while working this way that allows your life to flow and positive outcomes to develop.

Thought for the day!

By working with Self in the Second Order – Work think of one positive job you can you do tomorrow and do it.

Please record your experience

....

....

....

....

....

We started the beginning of this Chapter speaking about your memory and how it is needed and how it works with your ego personality states and then moved on to include the Self – Second Order – Work.

Working in the Second Order, helps with stress reduction. It also allows you to achieve the goals and to complete the projects you set yourself.

The Second Order is always productive. It is when students effectively study for exams, they are ready, they work hard to achieve the marks they want. They do not become distracted by trivia; their mind is on the job to be done. They are indeed working with their Adult ego personality state and the First and Second Orders of Self – Work. This thinking and action becomes a powerful combination for achievement.

It is the same for a surgeon or doctor performing a delicate operation on the brain, the surgeon is working with the First and Second Order of Self within the combination of Work.

There is more about this exciting discovery as you read the next two chapters.

First and Second Orders – Work

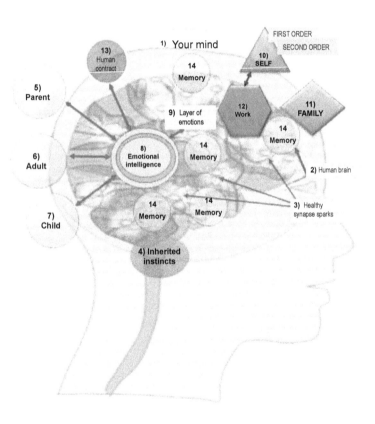

Your memories of different events allow you to recall the image or experiences you have previously had in your life. As you work now, and in the future, think, how can I use this information when I am working with Self in the First and Second Orders in my emotional intelligence and in my Adult ego personality state?

Thought for the day – SELF

From the reading you have done, you are becoming familiar with how your brain and mind work together. When understanding this human technology you have inside your head, you become more effective, understanding and finely tuned, not only to your own feelings and experiences, but also to those people you love, your family, and those people you work with.

Your Notes

....
....
....
....
....
....
....
....
....

The power of Self, working within the First and Second Order the Adult ego personality state and your memories

We are all similar, we each have a brain and mind but each of us use these human instruments and technology in different ways.

Your emotional intelligence works for you as do your Parent, Adult, and Child ego personality states. When you know how to operate these mind tools, you take control of your life, maintain a positive direction, and reach your goals.

You cannot escape from Self, it is there working with you 24/7 as this is so, why not learn to drive your Self and mind in a positive direction?

This learning contributes to:

✓ gaining personal confidence
✓ the availability to find solutions to problems
✓ the inner energy to face difficult times
✓ you have an understanding and know that difficult times pass, you know, you also gain great knowledge from the difficult times you experience.

Managing difficult times takes great amounts of positive energy, finding this energy, you must. Experiencing difficult times raises your awareness, this awareness allows you to minimise your stress levels and contributes to your wellbeing.

The brain and mind are great gifts we each inherit from our parents and ancestors. When you stop to think about this, would you like the gifts you hand down to your grandchildren and greatgrandchildren abused and not to be used properly? This is the power within the learning you are doing.

Your Notes

. . . .

. . . .

. . . .

. . . .

. . . .

. . . .

. . . .

. . . .

. . . .

. . . .

. . . .

. . . .

. . . .

. . . .

. . . .

. . . .

. . . .

. . . .

. . . .

. . . .

. . . .

179

Unmanaged
stress is a
time bomb
waiting to
explode!

Chapter Nine

The Third and Fourth Orders – Working with Self, Family and Work – Continuing the Story

It has taken many years of observing people in the workplace, teaching environments and in life that has allowed me to answer some of the questions I have running around inside my head.

This way of research is titled: observational psychology. In the realms of Psychology, it is also known as Behavioural Science. Science is a science because, as a scientist, I can use measuring tools in the form of numbers to measure outcomes. Through observation, and collecting data, human behaviour can be measured and used as a guidance tool for now and future generations. The science is complicated and relates to collecting numbers, crunching them, and looking for correlations.

From the past work I have done, this book has now become a culmination of years of observational research put together through words, and in some instances, models which take the shape of pictures. The purpose of the book is to make managing stress simple and easy to understand.

In the previous Chapters, we have looked at the First and Second Orders within each personality state of Child, Adult and Parent. Coming to this Chapter, I am speaking about the Third and Fourth Orders within the ego personality states mentioned.

Eric Berne's work of the 1940s and 50s has opened the door to many compelling questions about how our minds work under different circumstances within life's experiences.

Discussed previously were the First and Second Orders.

- **Self – First Order** incorporates planning, contemplation, the development of ideas and other positive thoughts you have about your life. You may take some time out to read, pray, quietly sing, recall the sound of falling rain, imagine a gentle river running or recite some poetry to yourself. This is an excellent Order for stillness of your mind, togetherness of your mind, body, and soul and to further contemplate your wellbeing – it is stillness, quiet and a time of one for Self. As individual's we can only work with Self – First Order in the Adult ego personality state.

Courtesy Jennifer Murray

- **Self – Second Order** is about action, getting things done, the development of projects, making sure the house is running properly, developing lists, running your business, teaching students, fixing the car, playing ball with the children, making a birthday cake, knitting a jumper, building a house, feeding the chickens and so the list of 'doing jobs' expands every day. Doing is how cities are built, science is developed for the benefit of humankind, hospitals are managed, fire fighters fight fires, pilots fly aircraft, ships sail the oceans and more. When we work effectively in the Self – Second Order, we work essentially with the Adult ego personality stage but can revert easily to the Parent or Child ego states in the different jobs we do. By reverting in this way, we become effective operators in the jobs we do. Both the Child and Parent ego personality states are eager to co-operate and all personalities work in unison, production, and the work to take place.

Overview: Self – Third Order

Moving into the Third Order within the personality states of Parent, and Child.

Your emotional intelligence and other connecting parts to your psyche may not be heard in this Order!

As I observed the inmates of both the young offenders' institution and the offenders in the jail in England; some of the offenders were continually angry and aggressive. I think this was the tipping point for me. I had read some of Berne's work, but I also had his suggestions of the Parent, Adult and Child in my head. The question I kept asking myself: *'why are some of these young men so angry when others are not?'* One young male stood out from the crowd – he was always angry and if he was not in trouble, he made trouble.

At this time, I was working on the children's books I write, I was also teaching, so I had enough work to keep me going, but still the questions persisted about anger with some of the young inmates in the offenders' institution.

It was at this time, I started to think, there must be more to each ego personality state than I realise. The Orders for each state have taken many years of thinking about but they must be there inside our heads and only become noticeable when we experience different situations or reactions to situations.

Self – Third Order

The Self in the Third Order is a stressful condition for both the mind and body. It is a time of tension, frustration, anxiety, anger, and annoyance for the individual experiencing this Order. This is the Order where people make decisions that have devastating outcomes for families, neighbourhoods, and communities.

This is the Order where negligence occurs, accidents happen, and innocent people are hurt.

Just recently we saw the devastation of the port of Beirut with the explosion and destruction of the seaport and surrounding suburbs. It appears that negligence may have played the greatest part in this. People working in the Third Order, for the most part, do not take responsibility for their action or lack of action and therefore, awful accidents happen.

Just as this is so, calculated destruction also takes place in the Third Order. The terrorist activities of 9/11 would have taken place while the individuals were in the Third Order. Also, civil wars, terrorism, murder, hurt and harm, all happen when an individual or groups of people come together in the Third Order. Added to this is the personality states of each of the perpetrator.

There are millions of stories of atrocities the world over and each atrocity has been committed through the calculation in the human mind and then the actions committed by the offenders.

The untamed mind of the perpetrator plays a sinister role while the individual works from the Child ego personality state and when working from the Third Order of their mind.

From the previous Chapters, you will be aware that, we, each, and every person, can drive their mind in the direction they choose. How you drive your mind is your decision, but each negative decision taken can carry severe penalties and outcomes.

The heightened stress of the induvial while working in the Third Order may be high and does the human body and brain no good. The sinister concoction of thinking and indeed, some pleasure, can and does happen in this Order.

It is difficult to mention pleasure while writing about the Third Order, but pleasure may come to some individuals when they commit atrocities. This pleasure may be short in satisfaction when accountability is thrown at individuals when prison sentences or punishment is handed down.

Self – Third Order – Child ego personality state

As I have previously said, allowing the Child ego personality state to take control while in the Third Order can produce sinister outcomes. A tantrum from a child, if not controlled in the younger years, may become aggressive and destructive action and behaviour when the child becomes an adult. As the child matures, so does the emotional intelligence of the child. Once bad behaviour is established early, this forms habits, the habits will become difficult to shift as the child goes from childhood to adulthood.

The Parent ego personality state may also play its part in the behaviour an adult can exhibit! When the Parent ego personality is authoritarian, it may encourage the Child ego state to continue its sinister pathway. Please note, when the Third Order is activated, the emotional intelligence of an individual may go into red or black; sinister thoughts and activities may be all the person, in this operating mode, can think about! In this Order the Adult ego personality state with reasoning, may be disconnected. Please see the figurative shape (number 8) of emotional intelligence below.

Self – Third Order – Family

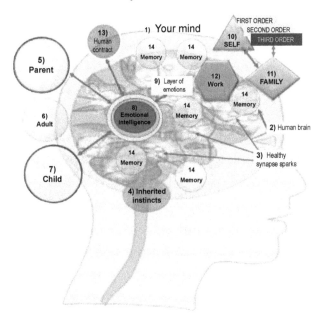

When the Self is in the Third Order Family, atrocities happen, and people suffer. It is the Order where domestic and family violence take place, it is the Order where family lives are taken.

Hannah Baxter

The story of Hannah Baxter and the murder of her three children in Brisbane, Australia, 2020 is one of untamed anger and revenge. It is the gruesome outcome of how a person can take, not only his life but the life of his wife and three children.[23]

Hannah had strapped the children into the car and was ready for the school run when her estranged husband jumped into the car and doused his children and Hannah with petrol, then set them on fire. The car became an inferno. Both Hannah and her husband survived the initial blast. Beside the burning vehicle, Rowan Charles Baxter, stabbed himself and died of his injuries. Hannah later died of her injuries while in hospital.

Emotional intelligence – Third Order

Your emotional intelligence also plays a big part if you allow your thinking to go into the Third Order. You can become trapped by your own thinking this is not necessarily an easy place to escape from. By previous negative thinking and actions taken, we can each go to the place of Rowan Baxter. This thinking is the place where a person can become involved with criminals, terrorists, and other peer group organisations. I have previously mentioned the Muck-Up days by the students, earlier in the book. Such behaviour needs to be stamped out; students in the high school

---

[23] Brittany Chain for Daily Mail Australia

setting also need to learn about how their mind works, if this is done, we may avoid such tragedies as seen in the case of Hannah Baxter and her children previously mentioned.

The power of the group, cult or following

As with many sinister situations, a commitment to the group, cult or following will be maintained by the 'fear factor' and the possibility, if found out a person is thinking differently to the other followers, retribution may be the result as in death in the most sinister of situations. All such thinking and actions interfere with your stress levels and the way you think and the actions you take.

Many people become involved with crime and other negative group activities because they are looking for belonging. People will modify their situation to meet different ideals to belong and feel connected.

It is essential to know and understand how you think, if sinister thoughts are within your head, please seek counselling and help.

The Third Order – Work

Working in the Third Order – Work. If an employee, business partner or other people connected to a business work within the Third Order – Child or Parent, it can cause major destruction to the business or organisation.

Working with such a mindset can be destructive, not only to the individual, but to an employer's investment in their business, customer or client investment and the money capital previously invested. In such instances, intellectual property investment may be stolen along with ideas and future planning of the business. Such is the state of mind of a vengeful employee or of a person who carries negative thoughts and ideas about another person's dream or accomplishment!

Vengeful activities

Being in the office refurbishment business is challenging and competitive. After many years of working for his boss, Dominic had been made a director of the company. Dominic worked well with the other employees. Working as a director, Dominic started to see how, 'money-on-the-side' could be made.

He would go out into the office blocks, in and around London, and give quotations for the work that needed to be done in different companies. He would then do an itemised quote, submit it to the office staff for costing and then the material and necessary funds, to complete the job, would be made available.

Dominic soon learnt, by the overordering of different materials, he could indeed, fund his own work in the same industry. This he did for many years. One day, an audit was done on one of Dominic's jobs and the discrepancies in costing and material needed to complete the job were identified. Further research had shown the level of embezzlement went further than on the material and money spent. Further to uncovering the abuse of power as a Director of the company, Dominic would submit refund documents, when paid, the funds would also end up in his pocket!

There are many stories in the business and working world like Dominic's story. Some people see the opportunity to abuse innocent situations and use the situation to commit theft of the very people who employ them!

Vengeful activities while in the Third Order – Work, also happen when people are fired or sacked from their employment. In the United States of America, this year, there were news headlines of the outraged, dismissed worker who had a shot gun and once leaving the premises returned to his previous employer and shot many of the remaining employees.

Such actions happen when people are in the Third Order – Child or Parent ego personality states. The Adult ego personality state within the person's thinking does not exist when such anger overtakes the thinking of an individual.

Managing and working with your mind is just one of the challenges we have in life. Many religious organisations have taught us about thinking and about how to use the mind for effective and positive outcomes. However, being human, and, in order, to grow and mature, we sometimes need to experience painful learning experiences. Even with this last sentence said, you still have the choice of going into the Third Order.

Your memory

As we each grow and mature, the memory collects both positive and negative pictures and information of past events, these are stored in your memory banks. These stored images or information do not normally erase themselves unless there is damage to the brain. If you have past negative images held in your head and you want them to go, they will not. However, the brain is of a forgiving nature and there are exercises that can be done to lessen the burden of a negative memory.

Your options

People commit atrocities, hurt and harm to other people but they have the choice to do or not do and to take the actions they take.

Self – Fourth Order

For my part, this is a refreshing part of the book. The Fourth Order is an Order of rebirth, life, freshness, and positive, growth.

Being in the Fourth Order – Self is a refreshing Order to experience, it is a time of being positively effective in your life. You have plans, goals, and accomplishment in your mind. Nothing deters you from the challenges you set yourself.

People can sometimes be hurtful in the words they say and the actions they take. Speaking from my own experience, if I had listened to the negative words spoken about my book writing and the development of my online bookstore, I would have stopped writing the books at the first hurdle, but I had a dream and that dream is now seen on my website. It is now twenty-one years later and still I persist with my dream.

Working in the Fourth Order

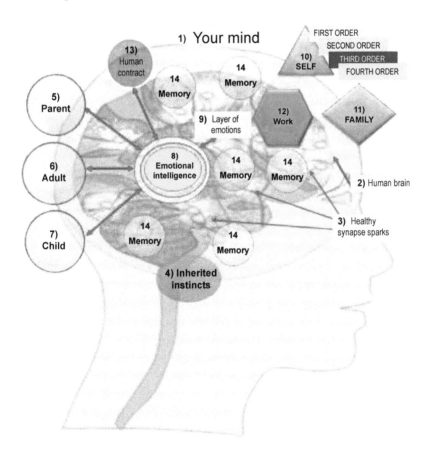

The Fourth Order – Self, in my own experiences, identifies itself when I have been through an experience that has allowed me to change and to become the person I am meant to be. Going through each ego personality state at different times in my life has allowed me to experience how I can change. I do not have to follow my emotions when I am hurt or angry, because experiencing emotions can give a false picture and distort reality.

When the Parent, Adult and Child ego personality states are working as they should we would see the Third Order as being detrimental and harmful to our health, wellbeing, and those people around us.

We each, have the ability, to by-pass the Third Order, but this cannot be done if we each, individually, do not know how to drive our mind in a positive direction.

The Fourth Order within Self may be elusive to some people, but with perseverance and continued positive mind work it can be achieved.

The sense of achievement when we work with Self in the Fourth Order is of accomplishment. Not only are we learning to effectively work with our mind, ego personality states and emotional intelligence but we have started to grow into the intended person with the purpose of life in our sights and the person we are meant to be.

The obedient servant – the human brain and mind

The human brain and mind are obedient servants and will only do what we give as commands to do. Living a life of accomplishment or living a life that is both good and kind is within us all.

As has been pointed out previously, we can so easily follow a wrong pathway if situations present themselves. Some people, despite their cruel and real-life experiences, remain in control of their thinking and actions. Many of these people are seen when refugees eventually make homes for themselves in different countries around the world.

When the Adult, Parent and Child ego personality states are balanced and work in conjunction with each other, and within Self, Family and Work life takes on a different role of growth and renewal rather than destruction and evil.

Under the most severe of circumstances, we can each work in a positive and constructive direction – working with the Fourth Order

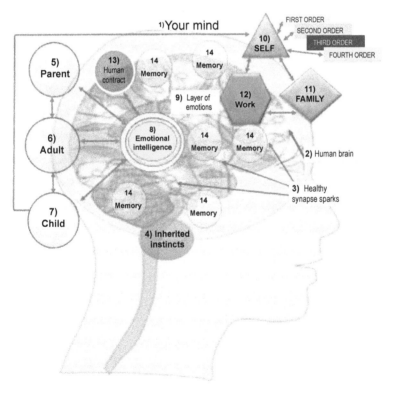

As said, we can each by-pass the Third Order within Self, Family and Work. Please look at the model on the previous page. You will see that the Third Order is completely by-passed by the ego personality states. The ego personality states remain of equal size and strength and Self, Family and Work are working in the First, Second and Fourth Orders, by working in this way, regardless of circumstances, you will stay on track and maintain stability in your life.

Like many other people, I too have had my difficult times. To find work and to start my life again, because of the financial recession in Australia, the loss of my business left me homeless. In order, to start my life and to find teaching work, I left Australia and re-settled back in England, the land of my birth.

Leaving my teenage children behind was the most difficult experience I have had, but I did it, in order, to start again. If I had not experienced my own heart breaking situations, I do not think I could write these books, nor would I have done the enduring years of research that allows me to draw on those experiences which now allows me to write about the subjects I write about.

Living in the Fourth Order

The Fourth Order is a place of growth and renewal, it is a place where you hear the birds singing in the trees, watch the flower buds unfurl, and see the fresh bright green of emerging fresh green leaves on the trees in the springtime. Renewal can take place through exercising, yoga, and other mind resting activities.

The marvellous brain and mind we each have inside our heads can sweep between our emotional intelligence, Self, Family and

Work within a nanosecond. Because of the power of the human mind and the speed at which it operates, the mind can easily shift gears as we hear the ice cream truck pull up outside the house, and think, *'I might go and buy an ice cream.'* By the time you reach the truck, you may have thought of the heading or words in the book for the next chapter you are writing; if you are a business owner, you may have thought of a good lead for your business and will contact them immediately you have finished eating your ice cream. You may be a company executive and while buying the ice cream for the children, think of the next policy to put into place that will allow for safety and accountability for the people managing Health and Safety in the workplace.

The Fourth Order allows for the progression forward in the accomplishments we want to make.

Thought for the day!

When you work in the Fourth Order – Family, what advantages can you see for yourself and the Family by getting to the Order as quickly as possible?

....

....

....

....

....

....

Thought for the day!

The Self, Family and Work in the Fourth Order can achieve many benefits. What positive, growth can you see in your life by working in the Fourth Order and what could you do to initiate changes?

....

....

....

....

....

....

Self and Family –

Second Order, Third Order and Fourth Order

Think of a time when you could have applied your First Order Self within the Family and write it down.

....

....

Think of a time when, because of misunderstanding, you could apply Self and the Second Order of Family and write it down.

....

....

The Third Order of Family may be difficult to come to grips with, so think about it – you may wish to come back later to do this exercise. How did you cope when you experienced this Third Order? Write it down when you are ready.

....

....

The Fourth Order is a time of Positive Growth; if you are in a life dilemma, reach out for the Fourth Order Family. Now think: 'How will you do it?' Write it down.

....

....

When you work with Self, Family and Work you have the advantage of knowing the Order you are working with – these advantages include:

- You can avoid a lot of negative stress in your life.
- See solutions to possible problems before they are problems.
- Be forewarned and ready, to take action, if needed.

Please take some time out, think about your emotional intelligence, your ego personality states of Parent, Adult and Child, then think about the Orders of First, Second, Third and Fourth. How can you make changes? Please work on your mind when you need to, after all, this book is about reducing stress but it is also an exercise of getting inside your head and understanding about you and who you are.

....
....
....
....
....
....

Your Notes

....
....
....
....
....
....
....
....
....
....
....
....
....
....
....
....
....
....
....
....
....

Unmanaged stress is a time bomb waiting to explode!

Chapter Ten

Getting Inside Your Head

The human head weighs about twelve pounds (5.44kg), this includes, eyes, teeth, brain, skull, and other necessary parts, including ears. The brain weighs about three pounds (1.36kg). The weight of stress only adds to the physical stress you experience. To aim to keep added stress out of your head and body is the mission of this book.

Getting inside your head

Reactivity vs proactivity

This book is essentially about becoming proactive in your life – you think action, before the action has taken place! With reactivity you take action after the action has taken place. Sometimes, being reactive is necessary. If for instance, you see a child in danger, you would react without thinking and put action into your movement to save the child, you do not think about yourself – just saving the child.

Proactivity – driving your mind

Driving your mind in a positive direction means weighing up the **pros** and **cons** to keep balance in your life. The mind you have working inside your head, as I have said, is the gear box you have and like all vehicles, the mind, to achieve your goals, and ambitions needs to be driven in a positive direction.

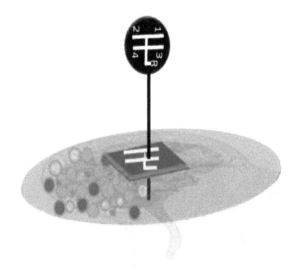

First gear

As in the First Order of Self, Family and Work it allows you to start on your journey. This is a time of thinking, stillness, and preparation.

Second gear

As in the Second Order of Self, Family and Work. Is a time of action. You move forward and take the right directions to either get the job done or do a large part of the job, you still have enough fuel in the tank to finish the project. You are managing your stress levels and successfully incorporate all the jobs, goals, or projects you have before you.

Third gear

As in the Third Order of Self, Family and Work. You are gaining speed, but you are not taking care, you may become reckless and out of control because you are not thinking clearly or proactively, you may also become aimless, cause an accident or get yourself into trouble.

Fourth gear

As in the Fourth Order of Self, Family and Work. You are cruising, driving within road speed limits and you can see your destination in sight. You may be driving to a new home, hobby or enjoying the journey. You may be looking at new horizons and new personal growth that is about to take place. This may include starting a new course of study, the first day of a new job with a promotion and more.

Reverse

When our lives go into reverse and we repeat the same actions only to receive the same negative outcomes, we know that we are making the wrong decisions and choices in the first place.

How many times do we get in the car, follow the map only to end up in a dead end? This is the same when our lives go into reverse – we can easily end up in a dead end. The only solution is to reverse out of the situation and take a different route.

Reverse can happen when we go back into relationships that does not fit with our personality. *'We give it another go…!'* only to allow that person to hurt us again. A similar scenario can be seen when people go back to a job they have left and return to the work only to find out that nothing has changed, the same negative cogs are moving in the same negative cog direction…!

Once you have decided on change, with the information you now have, make the changes to make your life better and reduce your stress. Change does include adjustment and adjustment takes time. Adjustment is also a time of transitional stress but it is good stress because you are on your own, life journey.

The goldmine inside your head

Through the years, and as we get older, we accumulate a great amount of knowledge, knowledge is worth its weight in gold and many people would like to own the knowledge you have inside your head.

Through the research and writing I have done over the years, my interest in our minds and brains still holds my focus, so now please let me introduce you to your mind made of gold.

Your mind of gold and the Centre of your Intelligence

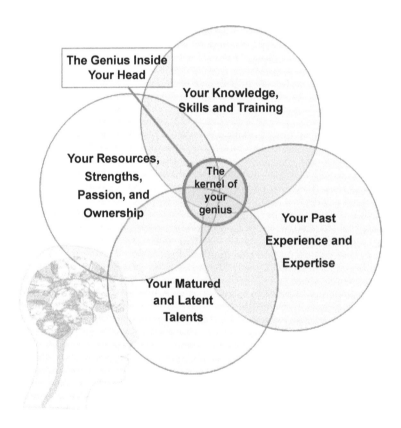

Many company directors, successful musicians and artists can be paid big incomes because of the knowledge or talent they have.

The kernel of your genius is where all of your experience, knowledge and learning cross-over, these include your:

- Knowledge, Skills and Training
- Your Past Experience and Expertise
- Your Matured and Latent Talents and
- Your Resources, Strengths, Passion and Ownership are there inside your head.

They are there and ready for use

Do not under value yourself. You have taken many years of your life to build the gold you have inside your head, now is the time to use it.

It is far more advantageous to look at your overall goals and daily jobs as a set of actions to take or words to speak than to sit and let life run out of control. Some people are used to writing lists, but some are not. The 'list writers' normally get to their goal because they have a plan of action.

Looking at stress again; without some stress in our lives, we would get nothing done – **Reducing stress**

1) **Positive stress** allows you to get the job done.
2) **Negative Stress** is destructive to your mind and body and needs to be controlled.
3) **Transitional Stress** allows you to go from one situation, action, or spoken word to another.
4) **Accumulated Negative Stress** is stress you have experienced over a long period of time.

5) **Post-traumatic Stress Disorder** (PTSD). PTSD can occur after experiencing or witnessing a major trauma.
6) **Acute Stress** is the experience and the feeling of a lack of reality, life is just an existence!
7) **Hypertension** is high blood pressure.

Like so many people worldwide, I do suffer with stress. I try to maintain my stress levels through breathing properly and exercise, but I can be caught out…

Starting at 1 from the opposite page.

1) **Positive stress** – allows you to make positive changes in your life. The Adult ego personality state in positive stress is productive, energetic, enthusiastic, keen, eager, raring to go and you have heart and endurance power in everything you do.

2) **Negative stress** – is destructive to you and your environment. It holds you back as your world appears to be dark and miserable. You want to make changes, but negative stress takes all your good, positive energy. You are left depleted with little to no energy to make the changes in your life you need to make. Negative stress may also show itself after a severe illness or with the breakup in a relationship. If this describes you, please seek professional help and support.

3) **Transitional stress** – works well with positive stress; it allows you to manage your life, create work for employees if you are an employer, take strategic action when needed, sit successfully for examinations if you are a student, create an effective marketing campaign for a good client, organise a

market day for the village fair and other projects that need leadership skills.

4) **Accumulated negative stress** – like negative stress, accumulated negative stress has been part of your life for a long period of time. Experiencing domestic violence may add to accumulated negative stress. You may have the feelings: I'm surrounded by this, I cannot breathe, I feel I am suffocating under this pressure and many other health depleting experiences while you try to cope with accumulated negative stress. If this is describing you, you will need to become proactive with your thinking and to prepare yourself for change.

5) **Post-traumatic stress disorder (PTSD)** – many people experience (PTSD), including children. It may show itself through sleep disorders, including nightmares and through exaggerated thought processes. Like other stress disorders mentioned in this book, PTSD is a condition that needs to be identified and the sufferer needs to have medical support and understanding. Like so many stress-related health issues, any form of negative stress is a real health condition that depletes the induvial of positive energy and is exhausting to live with.

Negative stress is a bombardment on the mind, body, and health of the sufferer. It needs to be managed and understood.

6) **Acute stress** – is stress that has persisted over a long period of time, or it may appear after a severe shock. When our son was diagnosed with Type One Diabetes or Juvenile onset Diabetes, I went into acute stress. To those people around me, I functioned as normal and seemed to manage the day-to-day

running of the home, attend my university lectures, tutorials, and seminars, but I knew I was not right. I did not feel right, I felt I was living in a non-reality existence.

7) **Hypertension** – is accumulated stress but it is far more dangerous than the stress I have previously written about. Until recently, I had not experienced hypertension but have now found out what it feels like after being diagnosed with the condition. Hypertension is high blood pressure that dramatically increases the risk of heart attack, stroke, and heart failure. My own condition was brought on by an external demand with my writing and the feeling I had no control over the situation. It shows itself with severe headaches, breathlessness and becoming lethargic.

I practise the recommendations I write about, but the stress I endured with the feelings of being out of control, was a condition I needed extra medical support with, this I urgently got through going to my doctor.

Please take immediate action if you are experiencing any the above negative stress conditions.

Through my own experience of stress, it has led me to research and write about this condition. I am sure I have mentioned many stress conditions that are not in the public forum, but they should be. We all need to have the mental tools that will allow us to drive our mind in positive directions. Managing stress in the Twenty-First Century should be incorporated into life education and other life-skill courses both in primary, high schools, and further education

LEARNING HOW TO BREATHE

When you feel stressed or daily activities and problems are too much to cope with, take just five minutes out of your day to do this simple relaxation technique.

Do the simple breathing exercises outlined below:

✓ *Breathe in through your nose – hold: count to 3*
✓ *Push the air down into your lungs – hold: count to 3*
✓ *Exhale the stale air through your mouth – to the count of three – then start the process again.*

By doing this simple exercise, you are creating a simple breathing feedback loop that works with you under any stressful or difficult situation.

Extracted from my Whispering Poem books – for relaxation and developing mindfulness – music and art therapy – A Treat For Your Senses.

More details about breathing further in this Chapter.

Extracted from my book: 'Go' Success is Yours

Managing stress – Work

Stress Guide and Monitor – In Work – record 1 – 10

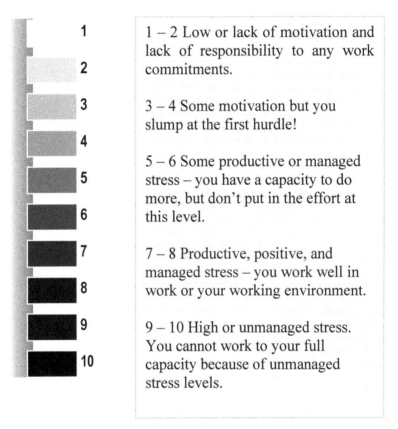

1 – 2 Low or lack of motivation and lack of responsibility to any work commitments.

3 – 4 Some motivation but you slump at the first hurdle!

5 – 6 Some productive or managed stress – you have a capacity to do more, but don't put in the effort at this level.

7 – 8 Productive, positive, and managed stress – you work well in work or your working environment.

9 – 10 High or unmanaged stress. You cannot work to your full capacity because of unmanaged stress levels.

With the Stress Guide above, you can adapt it to Self, Self – Family and other areas of your life.

The Stress Guide

1 – 2   Little to no stress – a perception there is little to nothing on offer in life – life is boring and un-eventful, so no extra effort is put into managing or doing anything about the situation. This type of reaction may also be an indication of depression. You may indeed think you are not stressed but you may be under stress because of your situation. Please seek professional help if this is you.

3 – 4   You have some motivation, there is some positive and transitional stress, but you slump at the first hurdle or challenge! Please look at the food you are eating. Are you eating processed food with a high number of food additives? If you are eating food that is not replenishing your body and is additive loaded, you may be experiencing a depression combined with low body and mind energy.

5 – 6   You have some productive and managed stress, you want to do more but may feel *'What's the use, I'm not appreciated anyway!'* This feeling could also lead to unmanaged stress in 9 – 10! When a person feels this way, it is wise to look for other work or to look at friend or love relationships. These feelings may indicate a depression, but with the above spoken about so far, please check your self-esteem.

If you feel your self-worth and esteem have been battered through difficult times, please do something that is just for you.

✓ Look into the mirror, smile, and laugh at yourself; when you do this, you release serotonin a happy hormone, you

213

will feel much better after this exercise. This will also reduce stress.
- ✓ Do the breathing exercise mentioned in this Chapter
- ✓ Walk in the park
- ✓ Sit and watch a river
- ✓ Look into the sky and see the birds flying
- ✓ Look at the flowers, landscape, or views around you
- ✓ Laugh with the children
- ✓ See the funny side of life
- ✓ Do some writing or drawing – you do not have to be an artist, but you may discover a lost or hidden talent through doing this…!

7 – 8   You have positive, productive, and managed stress. You work effectively, produce good or positive results, and may experience going into 9 but manage to bring your stress level down through breathing correctly.

9 – 10 You experience a lot of stress and your stress is unmanaged. Unmanaged stress may be caused through your perception of events. Learn to re-frame your experiences through working with your Adult ego personality state and with your Self in the Second and Fourth Orders within your emotional intelligence. When you feel ready, through meditation or breathing exercises go to the Self – First Order and work with this Order in 7 – 8 for as long as you can.

To add to your understanding of managing stress, please follow Meichenbaum's Stress Inoculation on the next page.

Meichenbaum (1972) identified that Stress Inoculation works in three stages:

First Stage: Cognitive preparation.

Second Stage: Skill acquisition and coping strategies including *thought restructuring*.

Third Stage: Application and follow-through.

Stress Inoculation

First Stage: Cognitive preparation. Cognitive simply means the way you think: do you think 'your cup is *half-empty or half-full?'*

Most people understand this saying: if it's *half-empty* there is an assumption that you are a pessimist, negative and establish negative thoughts in your mind by continuous negative self-talk and creative negative mental feedback loops[24] – such negative self-talk and feedback loops may include the thoughts:

- *'I will never have enough material goods in possessions or money!'*
- *'I will struggle for the rest of my life because I am not worthy of anything better!'*
- *'I cannot be a success in life or work because I keep telling myself this!'*
- *'I am too sick to make a better life', ('...though I am only sick because I assume, I'm sick!')*
- *'Oh, no, I couldn't ask for more – that's all I'm worthy of...'*

---

[24] https://psychologydictionary.org/feedback-loop

- *'This is my lot!'*

In the previous, you are making negative assumptions about your ability to do what you need to do to make your mind and body healthy – negative assumptions also reduce your pathways to mind and material prosperity. This thinking allows the release of destructive quantities of hormones such as cortisol and dopamine which adds to your negative stress.

Meichenbaum – his assumption being: *'... stress is caused by faulty processing of information...'* Your negative mental processing of the incoming information is further enhanced by your negative self-instructions.

For example: Because you did not pass the driving test last time, you convince yourself you will not pass it the next time you take it. This type of negative self-talk leads to:

- Self-destruction
- Poor performance
- Reinforces your negative assumptions about yourself and
- Unnecessarily high stress levels.

If your cup is *half-full* you are an optimist and have a positive mind-set; you think, act and work at the opposite end of the mental thinking spectrum of the person who has a cup *half-empty*. You, have the ability to create enough money, and material possessions, to give you a *comfortable*, or more-than-*comfortable* lifestyle.

When there is not an opportunity to do something or get somewhere, you do everything in your power to create the opportunity, for positive outcomes to comer into your life.

With a cup *half-full* mindset, you have faith in yourself and put in the work to see the rewards in the future. PAY IT FORWARD, I write my books with the PAY IT FORWARD, this means, I write my books with the intention of helping or supporting someone, somewhere in the world either now or in the future. At the time of writing a book, there is no upfront money payment, I do it because I feel there is a need in our world to do this.

When your cup is *half-full*:
- You see hurdles as *challenge*s as a necessary process of life.
- You have the confidence to *make something out of nothing.*
- You are prepared to move home, town, cities, or country to make your life work for you and possibly your family.
- You are not prepared to let a negative situation stand in the way – you always look for an alternative option or outcome to a problem
- Your stress levels can go up, but you are aware enough to make *changes* in your life to manage your stress.

When you work with your cognition, you are working with your thinking ability in **Self** and the First Order of your emotional intelligence. You are now aware, and to be fully functional you need to work with your emotional intelligence, Self in the First, Second and Fourth Orders, Family and Work.

Second Stage: Skill Acquisition and coping strategies including *Thought Restructuring*.

Thought restructuring

Skill acquisition and rehearsal involves attempting to replace old negative statements, negative self-talk: *half-empty* thinking with positive statements, positive self-talk to *half-full* thinking and working with positive, mental feedback loops!

Skill acquisition also means you put your mind and muscles to *work* and develop *new life-skills* which will contribute to your financial security and self-sustainability.

When you change the way you think, from negative to positive, you learn to reduce stress and therefore start to add quality and benefits to your life. To *change*, you need to adopt and *work* with *Thought Restructuring.*

Breathing properly and thought restructuring

- You will need to allow thirty to forty-five minutes to do this exercise.

- Find a place that is comfortable for you – a comfortable chair would be an advantage.

- Can you find a place that is softly lit and a nice place for you to sit?

- If you are in a busy location, travelling internationally by air, in a staff room, office or where there are a number of people move to the quietest place you can find.

- If you are having trouble with noise, you can set up a *white noise* barrier. A barrier is done by listening to soothing music from a CD, earphones or turning on the radio. The music eventually sounds out any other noise – the only noise you hear, is what you are directly listening to.

- Sit quietly, breathing in through your nose count to three and push the newly inhaled air down as far as possible into your lungs, then exhale through your mouth to three counts; do this as many times as you can. By doing this exercise, you are inhaling fresh, new oxygen and exhaling out old carbon dioxide. *You are inhaling the future and exhaling the past.* As you learn to breathe, say the words: '*…inhale the future, exhale the past…* '

- Use these sessions to get you into the habit of working with your mind and body this way.

- While doing the breathing exercises and when you are ready:

1) Relax your jaw – you will notice, when you are tense, how tight your jaw can become! Let your jaw just be – let it hang loose. Develop this habit: when you are falling asleep at night, let your jaw hang loose. This really works – keep it hanging loose; if you feel it tightening, relax it again and let it be loose. By clenching your jaw,

you are putting extra stress into your body, continue: '*…inhaling the future, exhaling the past… '* Hold onto your incoming deep breath as long as you can, then exhale.

2) Now think of your shoulders, can you feel the tightness in your shoulders and your neck? Let your shoulders drop – feel the ease as they drop. While doing the exercises you continue with your breathing – '*…inhaling the future, exhaling the past …'* Hold onto your deep breath as long as you can, then exhale. Follow these examples through with all breathing exercises.

3) With your hands and arms resting either in your lap or on the arms of the chair, let them go, let all of the tension out; wiggle your fingers and then let them relax breathing regularly. '*… inhale the future, exhale the past …'*
Hold onto your deep breath for as long as you can, then exhale.

Now, from your upper body to your lower body:

4) Relax your feet, wiggle your toes to make sure you are responding to the exercises – breathing: '*... inhale the future, exhale the past …'* – keep your feet relaxed making sure your toes are not tightly curled up – relax your toes.

5) Uncross legs, now relax the calf in your legs, do you feel your legs are getting or feeling looser? Keep going, relax and feel the looseness and the lightness in your leg

weight – let it happen. Continue with your breathing: *'....inhale the future, exhale the past....'*

6) Now relax your thighs in the same way as you relaxed your leg calf muscles and feet, let your thighs fall deeper and deeper into the chair.

Your breathing and your body are now in a lightly relaxed and peaceful state.

7) Once you have reached a state of calmness, imagine putting a warm blanket around your body or sitting by an open fire and let your body soak up its warmth.

Do not put a blanket around yourself or sit near an open fire; this is *mind-work,* and the essence of the exercise is to make your mind do the work. This work will keep you safe and *comfortable* in the future. When you repeat these exercises at regular times, your stress levels will reduce; peace of mind returns, and you can readily work with your Adult ego personality state.

A note: *if you feel you are not warm enough at the start of the exercise, before starting, add an extra layer of clothing.*

You can re-train your response to stress, but you cannot retrain your physiological or your autonomic system's reaction to stress. Despite this, you can retrain how you react to the symptoms of stress; this is the power of Stress Inoculation.

Third Stage: Application and follow-through. *'The final stage allows you to work progressively from a moderately-easy-to-*

cope-with situation to a more difficult and demanding condition.'
Meichenbaum et al (1977-1985).

When you are working in the Third Stage of Stress Inoculation, you are the person in the control seat. You learn to work with the environment, the conditions within the environment and the way you are going to react.

By adding to Meichenbaum's model of *Stress Inoculation* the knowledge of your Parent, Adult and Child ego personality states, your awareness of Self, Family and Work and the Orders you are working from within your emotional intelligence. By doing this, you have the mental tools to make quick and efficient adjustments to manage your life and the difficult life situations you may experience in the future.

Identify your work performance and stress levels

If for instance you know you are working from your Child ego personality state and you are not performing at work, you can see from the following:

In 1 – 2

If you are in paid employment, you are working from the Third Order in your Child ego personality state. This would show you are not committed to the work at hand. You have little to no responsibility, you may have a 'don't care' attitude and don't care whether you are employed or unemployed – you are not stressed by the work you are doing – you may feel the work is boring!

In 3 – 4

You are working with your Adult in the Second Order. You may want to do the work, but your skill base may need to be upgraded or you may need further training on the job. This lack of skills or training could shoot your stress levels to 9 or 10.

In 5 – 6

You are working between your Adult and Child ego personality states in the Second Orders within Self and Work. You have a commitment to the work at hand; you do what is required but no extra. You can do more if pressured – you do not face or want to face any new *challenges.*

In 7 – 8

You know you are working hard from Self – Second Order and you are in the Adult ego personality state, you will know from the guide you have managed stress and that you are working within manageable stress guidelines. You can equally face and take on new *challenges* if you are asked to do so.

In 9 – 10

If you know you are going into 9, become aware of how you are feeling, listen to your breathing and monitor, then take the action to get back into 8.

If you are working in Work and within Self – you may come from the Parent and Child ego personality states in the Second and occasionally going into the Third Order because of the stress you are experiencing and the possible anger you are feeling.

You may have a demanding manager, supervisor or employer who wants '*blood out of a stone*,' which you cannot give. You may supervise other people below you. You perceive there is a lack of fairness in the work environment and your stress levels appear to be out of your control.

If, however, you can identify where you are on the stress guide, you can manage your stress levels.

If for instance, you are in:

9 – 10 and you are working with Self in Work and know your stress levels are too high, you still have the work responsibilities, but now, you take action to reduce your stress level.

Other options:

- You may take your mind back to the Adult ego personality state, Self – Second Order and delegate more work to other people.

- Working from your Adult ego personality state, Self – Second Order, you set aside regular meeting times and modify some of your work methods, thus reducing your stress.

- If you come from your Adult ego personality state and work with Self in the Second and Fourth Orders in Work and within 7 – 8 on the stress guide, your output, enthusiasm and production are greater, your enjoyment of your work is increased and each day is filled with personal and job satisfaction. Even in facing *challenges,* the *satisfaction* of the *work* persists.

A technique in quickly managing stress: The Stress Guide has 10 levels; you have 10 fingers. Count your fingers and identify fingers 7 and 8; with your opposite hand hold onto those two fingers, do your breathing exercises. This technique quickly takes you to positive and transitional stress and allows you to manage even the most difficult of situations. Of course, your management of stress is enhanced when you understand *How To Drive Your Mind.*

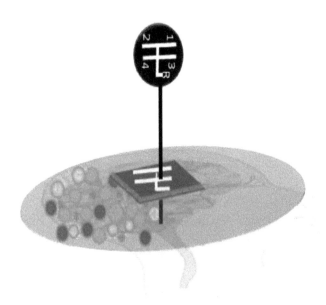

Thought for the day!

Untamed stress can be crippling to a person if they do not understand how the human mind interacts with the human body.

Stress can be managed but it takes time, discipline, and determination, but most of all, it takes you to understand how you react to different life experiences and the stress that is created by the experience.

Please take a moment to think things through and follow the exercise breathing suggestions on page 211. Recall your response.

....
....
....
....
....
....
....
....
....
....
....
....

Your Notes

....
....
....
....
....
....
....
....
....
....
....
....
....
....
....
....
....
....
....
....
....
....

Your gearbox inside your head – now you know you have it, there is no excuse not to use it!

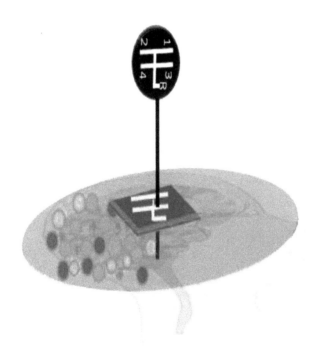

Case studies

- A traumatic journey – New Zealand Massacre
- Mike is determined
- The feel better box
- Damage to the cerebellum – Ataxic cerebral palsy
- Victoria
- Gottengen minipigs
- Different cultures of the world
- Wrong assumption – Robert – role confusion
- Victor Frankl's story
- Eve
- Hannah Baxter

Websites

Berne, Eric (1964) The Games People Play http://www.ericberne.com

https://www.thetimes.co.uk

https://www.feelbetterbox.com.au

https://neurologycp.weebly.com/case-study.html

https://www.dailymail.co.uk

Michael Winterdahl Scientific Reports www.medicalnewstoday.com www.nature.com

http://infomory.com

Dominic Lipinski/PA Lizzie Roberts, The Telegraph UK 3/9/2019

www.smh.com.au/national/nsw

Brittany Chain for Daily Mail Australia

https://psychologydictionary.org/feedback-loop

Unmanaged stress is a time bomb waiting to explode!